complete EARTHLY WOMAN

Embrace life's
lessons and
celebrate
personal
triumph

GENIE O'MALLEY

Sonra Enterprises
Mt. Shasta, California

Complete Earthly Woman: Embrace Life's Lessons and
Celebrate Personal Triumph © 2002 by Genie O'Malley

04–03–02–01   5–4–3–2–1

Authors of Unity Publishing
a company of Sonra Enterprises
575 Madison Avenue 10th Fl
New York, NY 10022
www.completeearthlywoman.com
www.authorsofunitypublishing.com

Book design by Sara Patton
Back cover copy by Susan Kendrick Writing

The suggestions in this book for self-development are not meant to
substitute the advice of a medical doctor or psychiatrist. It is essential to
seek the advice of such a professional in the case of any physical or mental
symptoms. The book contains only ideas and opinions of the author.

Publisher's Cataloging-in-Publication
(Provided by Quality Books, Inc.)

The Library of Congress has catalogued a previous edition as follows:

O'Malley, Genie, 1970–
     Complete earthly woman: embrace life's lessons and celebrate
personal triumph / by Genie O'Malley. — 2nd ed.
         p.   cm.
     LCCN 2001118387
     ISBN 0-9722980-0-2

1. Self-actualization (Psychology).   2. Self-realization.   3. Sexual
abuse victims — Rehabilitation.   4. Change (Psychology).   5. Breathing
exercises.   I. Title.

BF637.S4O43 2001   158.1
                                       QBI01-701049

Contents

Contents

A woman is a precious gift
to be protected as the
most sacred golden
light of love.
I am this precious light.
I hold myself in my own arms,
in love with that which I am,
a woman.
I give myself to each person,
each relationship
only where I am nurtured
as this precious gift.

෨ ෨ ෨

Acknowledgments

Rajmar
Circling the sun within a heart
of tranquility—thank you for the
sacred spiritual contract of our union.
Thank you for a love that allowed
me to breathe and allowed
this experience.

Jasmine & Joshua
A rainbow filled my life for
nine months and when I
found the pot of gold—two hearts
of gold emerged—radiating
ancient wisdom and love.
God thank you for the rainbow.
God thank you for the pot of gold.
God thank you for the sacred hearts.

Mom
Thank you for being the vehicle
of this life.
Thank you for your spiritual grace.
May your heart explode to the melody
of universal love.

Rose
Within my life you sit upon
the altar and within my life
I have inhaled your essence.
This essence a gift within the creation
of the Complete Earthly Woman.
May you now inhale
her essence—your true self.

James
May you inhale truth,
courage and the knowing
to seek your ultimate self.

Nana & Pa
The yellow daisies are smiling.
Thank you for believing that
in the darkness the light would shine.
Your faith took me to the light,
you kept me alive in the depths of pain
and nurtured in the depths of grief.

Dad
In golden light you sit upon a
mantel of forgiveness,
thankfulness and acceptance.

Stuart
May you honor the love
in a new life.

Acknowledgments

Jane, Kathi, Mary-Jo, Liz,
Sara, Anne and Denise
Thank you for allowing your hearts
to attune to the light and release
of the Complete Earthly Woman.
What a sacred group of women
set forth the essence of the
Complete Earthly Woman
through color, word and knowing.

Horst
In guidance of the Divine Mother
I was taken to the door of your ancient
Wisdom. Thank you for opening
the door and seeing the beauty
of the Complete Earthly Woman.

Dr. Hirsch
Thank you for seeing the essence
of the Complete Earthly Woman.

Acrabar
Thank you for the presence of nature
and the gifts of self-realization.

Thank you for appearing from my wardrobe.
Thank you to a saint.
Thank you violet ray and golden box.
Thank you Mother Earth
for taking me home

To all souls who pass in and out of this life
may you merge within the essence of self.

If you were told a secret
that all you had to do
is to take your miseries and
exhale them . . .

Inhale all you feel to be your
most empowering self,
would you do it?

Then do so.
It is that simple.

No need to study.
No need to learn.

Just accept who you are.
Believe in yourself.

Be brave when you meet all of you.
Love yourself,
exhale,
let go!

What's next?

Inhale within your heart
. . . truth, beauty, you.
Complete Earthly Woman.

$\mathcal{I}$ntroduction

I introduce this book to you as your friend—a friend who is saying open your heart to what you feel is pain and embrace yourself as a divine woman and your own master of self-transformation. This book offers a technique that will nurture the pain, the abandonment and the misunderstanding, transforming your sadness, confusion and longing into your most empowering aspects of inspiration, happiness and love. I know that in both the uniqueness and like-mindedness of this story you will be inspired to invoke changes and self-improvements that will both transform your thinking mind and empower your heart. Invoking gifts of self-transformation through believing that you deserve to exist as your most empowered self, finally setting free this empowered self from the ancient inner beauty that exists within.

When I first experienced that there was a movement of energy within me encouraging me to change, to locate inner beauty, I excitedly moved forward. I yelled out, "I know that I am worth it!" For the first time in my life I felt special, and surrendering my life to truth and changing my priorities to seek truth has been simple. That is what the self-transformation program within this book is for; to empower the action of simplicity within your life, your intuition. To invoke your personal healing path, where you are consistently determined to experience and merge within your truest, clearest and most pure aspect. Where you invoke values of love to pour forth from your heart as a constant, abundant flow of self-love.

This flow of love will transform your environment, relationships and existence into a divine reflection of your inner beauty. In the journey that we will take together through the following pages, you will become your inner beauty through consciously accepting the divine universal knowing that speaks through your heart as a most ancient master guiding your way. In my experience, witnessing this ancient energy has been amazingly entertaining to the thinking mind. It is happily sitting by watching a performance of the soul. Through the action of faith and by surrendering to this divine guidance in the past five years, a dance of the soul has wooed, tamed and captivated my ego. It has educated my mind on all inner transformations taking place and physical connections to the specific changes, as well as re-creating my thought processes. Through both accepting and understanding my own transformation, I know that we all have the ability to transform our lives into spiritual action. By seeking this change we receive our spiritual gifts. We begin to finally understand who we are and what life is here to teach us through the guidance of higher wisdom.

I have seen that we attain this type of support from the mind and awaken this level of understanding through one simple process. Self-Belief. Without self-belief, inner transformation is almost impossible. If you fail to believe in yourself, you will fail to identify with your spiritual wisdom, and the gifts of self-transformation. If you do not believe in what you feel, you will fail to see your truth.

In this moment, if you feel that you are experiencing a lack of self-belief, here is where you can completely nurture yourself and experience the empowerment of self-belief. Within the ancient wisdom of the Complete Earthly Woman you will be encouraged to hold hands with "you." To smile at yourself and courageously face your life and your past experiences knowing that you are a spiritual warrior and a true earthly woman.

When diving into what made me tick, I witnessed within my subconscious that my fears eventuated from a lack of worthiness that created an acute failure to believe in myself. I was constantly fearing what I would lose: my future, my attachments, who I thought I was and a great deal more encompassing similar negative suggestions or criticism. However, no longer. Today, since taking the road to conscious living and opening my heart to actively integrate with my soul, I am experiencing the ultimate love with myself and others. I am balanced emotionally, mentally and physically, and every day I am consciously striving as a spiritual warrior to master every part of me. A spiritual warrior I have become while writing and practicing the techniques of conscious breathing outlined within this book. Today I am free of negative interpretations and outcomes within my life. I understand my life and the purpose of this life. I do not hang on in fear of change. I am open and accepting of change. My life is an expression of this ultimate freedom.

In the process of writing this book I have been living each word. Unveiling every thought, reaction, expectation, experience and betrayal that created any dysfunction in my life. I began to recognize the experiences that had removed me from my inner beauty and believing in who I "truthfully" am — a soul on a physical journey. A physical journey as a woman. I see now that the duty to this woman is to honor this woman as a divine expression of the ultimate mother—the radiance of Mother Earth.

To allow the soul to nurture my role as a woman by filling my life with the highest teachings, guidance and light. This happens only when we are able to identify that it is vital to live the life of a woman as a Complete Earthly Woman. Consciously connected and consciously contributing to life.

In the beginning, writing this book was self-discovery; today it is dedication. It is a sacred opportunity to give inspiration, support and proof that beauty can shine from within the cloudiest diamond. A childhood of sexual, mental and physical abuse created an adult drug addict, addicted to denial. A girl with no boundaries. I was obese, depressed and suicidal. My life had been created from painful interpretations and memories. A life in which I continually experienced what had terrified my inner child until this day—the day that I now exist as inner beauty.

Available within the process of conscious breathing and seven invocations are the initiations for a sacred life as a Complete Earthly Woman. These are the final steps that are unveiled here on this journey to self-empowerment. The final steps I have taken to triumph from misery into magnificence. You will see that the physical body, your mind, your emotions, your relationships and your lifestyle are to be worshipped as a sacred temple in which you reside as a woman. You will take all that you are and allow it to shine as a temple of wisdom and nurturing love, inviting only "goodness" from others to sit within your temple—*your life.*

It will be through both meeting and knowing your own beauty that you will allow the love of others into your life. This magnificence will be empowered through your capacity to access the unconditional love you have for each and every experience within your heart. At the completion of this book you will be invited to take "conscious" residence within your temple—*your life*—and allow your heart to be the "welcome home" for all. Fearlessly, you will seek truth within your life.

In this moment is the choice to be empowered through the beauty and action of unconditional love and to live as the true gift behind the beauty of being a woman, a Complete Earthly Woman. Knowing and understanding that your life is the learning center for the soul will show you that your *life* is to be treasured as a gift—a gift to humanity. I invite you— through the inspiration of my own transformation—no matter how deep or how shallow the wound, nurse it. Allow yourself to heal and allow yourself to shine. Now is the opportunity to move consciously into the heart through conscious breathing and belief in what awaits within. Welcome to the chamber of ancient love within your heart, where you reside as the Complete Earthly Woman.

ॐ ॐ ॐ

$\mathcal{F}$inding Yourself in a World of Responsibility

Life is a journey of learning
Which can be seen simply as soul growth.

Welcome to the sacred journey within, to the ancient sanctuary of the Complete Earthly Woman. In this moment you begin a sacred journey within the heart, where you will experience freedom and safety by living as a truly satisfied woman. Your life will transform into a constant flow of love —a romance within yourself. Imagine a life in which you no longer judge yourself, but one in which your highest level of understanding consistently empowers your self-esteem. Imagine living the experience of pure joy abundantly filling your heart, the essence of your life flowering into the most magnificent rose of light. Where you exist, simply as you, minus the hang-ups, letdowns, harsh experiences, expectations of others and disappointments with love.

This is what can truly happen to you through igniting your flame of purification and continually placing every aspect of yourself that you want to change into this flame. You will turn past burdens into the sacred ash of transformation. Taking your tears and turning them into golden droplets of self-realization and sacred wisdom. Surrendering your tears to the golden voice within your heart, surrendering all that you know you need to change.

I encourage you wholly; use this book—this experience—to let it all fall away. Look at the time we will spend together as the time in which you will consciously re-create your life through inhaling who you feel yourself to be.

Invocation of the Complete Earthly Woman

Let us create a moment of silence. Begin by focusing on your breathing, witnessing each in-breath and out-breath. As you become aware of your breathing, it slows down and becomes a steady, calm, connection to your inner peace.

In this moment I invite you into your sacred union. I ask you to create a picture of you as a truly empowered woman. See her appear radiantly glowing. Feeling relaxed and calm within the mind you see her, and you humbly thank her in appreciation for coming forward and showing you your truth. In her presence you see your own inner beauty and your self-empowerment. Seeing her in this moment, consciously controlling each breath, you experience a peaceful inner connection. With each breath connect yourself to her. Feel her as you breathe in this moment.

She is calm, peaceful and very, very present. In your heart thank her for coming forward and inviting you into her sacred life, which is becoming the life that will be yours. A life whole and complete. Continuing to deeply inhale you see her, and through your breath you merge with her. Inhale into her presence. Inhale her into your thinking mind. Inhale her into this moment. Each thought you have that discourages you from this experience, exhale it.

Continue to breathe . . .

Focus on letting go of all resistance you may be experiencing from connecting with her. Align in complete wholeness with each controlled inhale and let go with each controlled exhale. As you breathe deeply your heart is warm. You have inhaled into your True self. Welcome.

Through your participation in this conscious breathing exercise you have integrated the presence of you — your empowered self—into your breathing. Throughout this book you will further empower this connection, but in this moment know that you have met. Through the action of your breathing you are acquainted and aware of your coming together. Your experience has begun. The steps you have taken have introduced you to your inner female truth, the Complete Earthly Woman. She will guide you through what you need to dissolve within different aspects of yourself that represent misinterpretations of your life. She will reeducate your mind, teaching you how to identify with the play of the sacred journey of your soul. Together you will take painful memories, desires for happiness and the search for self and create a life that is harmony, balance and highest understanding.

In the arms of the Complete Earthly Woman you will enter the Garden of Eden within your heart, where she will nurture you through conscious breathing as a divine loving mother. After your sacred purification of the mind and purification of negative programming you may choose to invoke the seven initiations of the Complete Earthly Woman (Chapter 11), which will take you step by step into a life as a Complete Earthly Woman.

On the last breath of this book you will have made the

connection to re-creating your life. Inhaling your new life and exhaling your past experiences. In the acceptance of change and with a thank you, you will let go. In the nurturing awareness of joy you will take on and connect to the true you. You have begun to seek the Complete Earthly Woman, and in seeking "ye shall find."

Sharing a Life

At this point I will share with you my credibility in writing this book. I was born in 1970 into a young family. My mother left my father when I was just a few weeks old. He was an aggressive, violent husband to my mom, and he became a heroin addict shortly after they separated. He then sexually abused me from age three to six. This betrayal shut down my association to the role of being a child.

Betrayal and distrust were set up in my psyche, and as an adult I created repeat patterns of this behavior throughout my life. Shortly after my parents separated my mother met my stepfather. Initially he was very kind to me and definitely encouraged me to rely on him as a father.

My next tragedy occurred at the age of eight, when two teenage boys sexually attacked me on my way home from school. This was especially traumatic for me, because I had only been at the school a short time and we had moved from the country to a major city. This final destruction dictated my life from the age of nine to fifteen, when I felt tormented by people in my life. Their lack of understanding of who I was and their ignorance of my pain collapsed my heart.

They did not know that my inner child had been sexually abused. From within me she looked at them begging for safety. They looked at her in ignorance. My experience with them tore apart the prospect of me ever developing into a healthy young woman. Even though they could not have known, inside I felt abandoned and rejected.

My parents' youth and their being locked within their own experiences made it difficult for them to see my truth as through their challenges they struggled to see their own.

By the time that I was thirteen my parents' marriage took a different turn. My mom spent a great deal of time trying to keep her marriage together. My stepfather was a man who fluctuated from overwhelming kindness to overwhelming aggression. He was unfaithful to his marriage and cut off from the wounds he created within us all.

My mother put a great deal of energy into keeping the "boat above water." To her, anyone else's issues had to be their own. She did not have the mental or physical energy to connect to whatever I was experiencing.

Our communication breakdown finally hit such a critical point that in a violent argument I left our family home. My stepfather was indignant and said that I was crazy. My mind behaved as if they had persecuted it. I looked at them as if they had betrayed me.

My saviors at this time were my grandparents. They seemed to know me. They were accepting. In so many ways they said I was worthy to receive love. They have believed in me every day of my life and constantly affirmed to other members of my family that I am a good person. My grandfather often suggested to me that I go within myself and cease seeking love from people, even if they were family. Especially those who did not want to give it, who did not even love themselves. He was right.

When we had innocent conversations in the backyard at

the apple tree, I never imagined that my grandfather was speaking from such an empowered state of consciousness, from such an open heart. My grandparents proved to me on more than one occasion that they loved me unconditionally. It was when my grandfather passed away five years ago that I began to seek change. It was at this time that I experienced on a few occasions what I know today to be open guidance from my intuition.

Today, my grandmother is a true best friend. My knowing says that we will never lose within our hearts our sacred bond. The divine respect and admiration I hold for her in my heart has always been abundantly nurturing. She was often ridiculed by certain members of my family for allowing me into their lives. Members of my family saw me as some kind of mental freak who was depressing to be around, living the play of some self-created melodrama. They never tried to understand why I had such acute pain. In pushing me away through their ignorance of my pain, I began to choke with grief. Shaking within, traumatized and alone in my sadness, fear and mis-interpretations. Their comfort in judging me protected them from any responsibility to themselves and their own actions. They did not have to accept how they felt about me. They did not own their responsibility to me.

Then one day my grief was seen and sadness nurtured. It was the day that a light exploded within my heart and blinded my vision. In focusing on this light within I have realized an abundance of truth and transformed pain into self-love. Today I know that my environment was provided for my soul growth. In a sense, those who seemed to hurt me most have been my greatest spiritual teachers, as I am theirs. I do not dislike them in any way. I truly honor their participation in my life. I give them love within my heart, and I send them bouquets of love often. To protect their feelings I will not deny the truth, because healing can only come from truth. I climbed a mountain of grief, pain and mental torture to turn my life around. I left home suffering acute depression, suicidal, with no self-esteem and a drug addiction.

Today, I pray within my heart that my family use the love that I have for them, the respect that I have for our experience and the humble way that I accept our experience as a light to heal and transform themselves. This is all I can give them. This honest, truthful, loving intention is the most empowering gift I can give.

Why Am I Here?

What do the ancient masters tell us? That we choose this life. We choose our parents and the lessons and circumstances that we face in life. When I first heard this I had great difficulty in grasping the concept. My first reaction was, "Yeah right, I asked to be sexually abused and for all of the other experiences of betrayal and abandonment." It took me time to integrate my life's purpose, to accept that I had chosen all of my experiences—both within my family and through my own actions. However, after conscious, spiritual self-development I can sincerely say it has been a life well-chosen. For even though I spent twenty-six years of my life trapped in the mind of a victim who had not experienced true nurturing, and carried the emotional and physical scars of sexual abuse, today, my life is filled with an abundance of universal love—a love that explodes within my heart on a path of service to my children, my husband, all women—humanity.

I know from experience that in helping another become empowered after an experience like sexual abuse and other traumatic experiences and to finally lay the victim to rest gives life a new meaning. Life today is an insightful expression of sincerity, compassion, forgiveness, pure love and joy.

I am telling you this because I wish to show you in as many ways as I can what I am experiencing as my life today. Through conscious breathing and the initiations of the Complete Earthly Woman I have healed deep wounds. I was stricken with pain at many times in my life—pain that I can only speak of today because I can in no way feel it. I still live life as the beholder of my experiences; however, I do not live life as a victim to these experiences. I have taken my experiences and turned them into a positive tool of life, all of my transformation emerging from within.

My spontaneous process of self-transformation was at times empowered by both my financial position and my inability to travel due to my health. I was not able to attend workshops, seminars or retreats, due to my commitments and a lack of financial resources. The only place available for me to go was within. I am not saying that the resources of workshops, seminars and retreats are not a significant step on the path of self-transformation. They are. They guide you into meeting others and identifying with avenues of self-transformation. However, from my experience, at times there was a need to be alone. In the silence of being alone I did not take on another's interpretation of change but assimilated my own.

So know that if you are financially restricted, opening the heart does not necessarily cost money. If you are not financially limited, remember to take time out to be alone. It takes courage to spend time alone; this courage is what will empower self-belief and intuition.

Courage to Seek Change

My motivation for writing this book, which is filled with the true beauty of the woman, was initially created through my need to overcome negative interpretations which turned into mental imbalance as the consequence of sexual, emotional and physical abuse. Through the sacred process of the Complete Earthly Woman I have transformed personal grief, sadness, acute depression, physical disease, obesity, asthma, alcoholism, drug dependency and personality patterns of self-sabotage and self-hatred into Self-Love.

Through the process of the Complete Earthly Woman, courage is provided through the knowledge, forgiveness, strength, love and wisdom that flows from the abundant source of healing energy that is available within us all. I accomplished this change simply by making the inner connection to the heart, our True self—the soul—chaperoned every step of the way to merge into the sacred wisdom of the Complete Earthly Woman.

To be a woman can be a blessed experience when you align to the inner miracles and beauty of nature. Inherent within women are energy patterns similar to those of Mother Earth. Our most precious female gift is our capacity to nurture all aspects of humanity. The sacred law of this capacity to nurture is to focus first on nurturing ourselves through the process of self-transformation so that we may offer both clarity and integrity to those we are blessed to nurture.

Because of our inner connections, women do not need to seek love outside of themselves. Within us all is an abundant resource of Mother Earth's intelligence—our connection to self-love.

Unfortunately, women have in some ways suppressed this quality, the nurturing female beauty. It is because of this denial of the female self that different diseases and disharmony have and will continue to present themselves throughout the reproductive system of the female body and the general health and well-being of women.

If at any time you suppress the true abundant flow of love that should flow through your womb, you could experience either physical, emotional or mental anxiety. This comes from blocking the flow of humanity within. This does not mean that all women are here to birth and raise children. It simply means that to be empowered as a woman you must locate the aspect of self-nurturing within your womb. Give birth to yourself. This will enable you to nurture all aspects of yourself and others through the action of higher wisdom. You will successfully nurture others by letting go of your expectations of them and their behavior.

With courage, strive to reach the companionship of yourself, knowing that all relationships outside of your own inner experience are a further blessing that you receive along the path of self-love. These relationships show you who you are and where you have to grow. Accept all of the experiences that you have had in your life. Thank the experience and the participants. Know that every experience you have had is stored in your sacred female center and has been a stepping-stone on your path of self-discovery. Invoke the courage to experience and transform what you have stored on a cellular level within your womb. Cross the bridge of self-doubt into the heart of complete wholeness.

Chapter 1

I encourage you to take the time to identify with everything you seek to release and change in your life. Then inhale into your transformation, guided by your heart. Accept all your circumstances as highest teachings. This will allow you to accept each experience as an action of love. Divine love. What is divine love? It is not necessarily everything we want to hear. It is not necessarily chocolates and roses. It is the expression of Truth. This truth comes through our experiences and relationships that allow us to identify with aspects of ourselves, which at times does not always appear to be a pleasant experience. From all experiences and relationships you can learn about yourself and how to further empower your life, as they encourage us to identify with the sacred steps of self-transformation: truth, self-love and forgiveness.

If you are a woman with responsibilities, either as a mother, a career woman, or a partner, I am sure that you are saying at this point, "Sounds great, but where's the time? How do I fit practices of conscious self-discovery into a life of diapers, breastfeeding or career?" From the washing to the meals, where's the peace and freedom found in a life filled with responsibility, especially the type of responsibility from which you cannot simply walk away?

In the very moment of writing this chapter I am living the responsibility of being a mother of two children, one four months old and the other nearly three. In this minute our four-month-old son is crying for his third breastfeed of the morning, and our daughter is standing at the bottom of the bed looking at me holding scissors and glue as if to say, "What are you doing in here alone? We have to play, mom." Right in this moment however, the calling of self-transformation is very strong, and it says that I owe it to these beautiful souls to find myself and let go of what bogs me down. So I do it. I experience in all of the exhaustion and chaos, the responsibility to honor my commitment to them and in return I am blessed with an inner strength for me.

Healing Every Minute of Every Day

I know enough at this time in my life to see that if my children need my time, my relationship needs my healthy, loving participation, and I need to honor my inner awakening, then I combine them all and do them together. But where to find the time? In my busy life I must be able to obtain inner silence and identify and surrender issues any time of the day. This is why I know that the process of conscious breathing is the perfect balance to the way of living that is outlined here and is incredibly empowering to a person living in a family situation or simply in a hectic life.

Through the practice of conscious breathing and invocations outlined in this book, you ignite your capacity to transform the thinking mind, the emotional interpretations and the physical body at any time of the day or night.

To overcome the experiences that have impacted your life you must relentlessly shine the light of transformation on your thoughts because . . . your thoughts create your life! Our entire lives and experiences are a reflection of our thoughts and our inner view. When re-creating our lives, good thoughts will empower our outer lives to further enhance our inner connection.

Being disciplined in your thoughts is the greatest service to humanity. No amount of community service or good deeds can replace the action of unhealthy thoughts or speaking unkindly of another. The most frequent trick I have witnessed the mind play is when it feels it can speak unkindly of another because it thinks it is concerned. It puts another down, noticing and pointing out their faults, because it claims to be concerned for another's well-being. Well, concern is not an excuse to not look kindly or not see only the best in another. If you cannot see the best in a person, do not look to see anything else. If a person demonstrates behavior that is not an action of love, then give that person love for their ignorance. Ask your heart that they identify with their ignorance and cease to act unkindly toward others. Give the person love for the pain they must be experiencing within themselves by not owning who they are and transforming their lives. In the pursuit of transforming yourself from all negative programming try to love all; otherwise you will fail to master your own transformation. Everything you do will be in vain and will not manifest for you in its truest capacity, and this will create disharmony both within you and around you.

Mothers are not the only ones who struggle to find time—all of us do. I speak of motherhood as an example, because this is my experience at this time. We all have many duties to perform in life, many interests and responsibilities. The process of conscious breathing is suited to everyone, because it fits into every situation. It is as simple as breathing and thinking, things we do every minute of every day. Inner transformation will also be empowered in the sense that you are able to consistently release patterns within each experience. You are not required to collect your experiences from your day and then relive them when you sit down quietly at a chosen time (even though sitting quietly at times and connecting to past experiences through visualization and conscious breathing is recommended for overcoming them). The main practice and benefit here is that you are consistently transforming your thinking mind by first identifying with behavior, then releasing the behavior with conscious breathing and transforming the behavior through conscious breathing and invocation. In my own experience and my experiences with others, "owning yourself—spots and all" is a pattern of thinking that will very quickly drive you along the path of self-transformation when we finally embrace all that we have experienced and all that we are.

Initially, when beginning this practice, you will have to put in the time and consciously listen to and purify your thoughts, but it will quickly become a natural way of being. In a short time you will hear yourself questioning your motives, your fears, your obstacles and all that does not flow in your life. You will spontaneously take a deep breath and blow it all away.

So when you are carrying a mood swing that bubbles for attention and has been triggered by a situation that you are dealing with, let it go. Exhale it, and inhale the warmth in choosing what is right for you and what is not. It's that simple. In seeing your issues you will become a better person. You will cease the selfish attitude that people deal with you, whatever your behavior. You will consciously heal yourself and will only give others your divine best, offering your values and not your grievances.

When I breastfeed I let go in my breathing all of the frustration that a mother will experience at different times due to being tied down. When I make love with my partner I exhale my fear of sexual intimacy, and I inhale the beauty of love that exists within that moment. After I make love I exhale any self-hatred or confusion about sexuality based on my experiences of childhood sexual abuse. I exhale any issues the inner child has with intimacy that she may be reflecting within my mind and that I will receive as thoughts of myself. When a person is rude to me, I exhale my judgment and I inhale self-love. I never let an opportunity pass by to own my response to a situation and let it go. After a while you cease having to let go and begin to witness an innocence and purity in your thoughts. Your actions manifest this purity and innocence, and from this your life will turn around. You will see and be comfortable knowing that life is a process of unveiling the real you.

In consciously transforming yourself, this inner beauty that you seek will become your life. Determination is a vital key in the success of this technique. Just discipline the mind long enough, and re-creating your life with conscious breathing will become a natural flow of thinking and living within your life.

It took me some time to adjust to the principle that the responsibilities in my life make me strive even further along the path of self-transformation and that I must be disciplined to access time for practices that empower my self-transformation. Every spare moment that I get for myself is precious, and I need to use this time wisely. Identifying with this makes me strive for self-transformation. You will not lose out to laziness when you seek with discipline to attune your life to the guidance of your inner voice. When you are living your life alone (for example, outside of a relationship or without children) you have the freedom to allow moments of silence to pass, because there are many moments of silence. Therefore, when you are alone it is best to discipline yourself so that you are consistently seeking silence to practice self-transformation.

Discipline is a measure of your belief that you are the beauty outside the burden of the mind. This burden is magnified and intensified when we are living a stressed, hectic life. Seeking a spare moment is vital to invoke the person within—the woman of peace, wisdom and courage. It is best, therefore, to surround yourself in both discipline and healthy responsibility. In speaking of healthy responsibility I refer to responsibility that mirrors the healthy aspects of you. This responsibility does not drag you down or overstress you but constantly challenges you to be your most positive, healthy self.

There was a time in my life when I was alone. From the experience of being alone and consciously seeking change in myself I can say that there is no excuse not to change. Especially when you are single, there is no reason not to discipline yourself in every aspect of your life. You have ample time to find your inner silence. It is a victim of hard times that resents being alone. Identify with the truth—that if you are alone you asked for it—as an aspect of your personal growth.

Use it wisely, so that when you do attract other people into your life you only attract what you strive to become—positive and consciously moving into your heart. When I was alone I chose to be alone, separating myself from others and my family. I chose this after realizing that in their company I was already alone.

It was at this time of my life that I fell in love with myself. I met me. I accomplished this by listening to myself and consciously breathing and shifting all perceptions and interpretations of my life that were not serving my self-esteem, my physical health and my overall existence in a positive healthy way. I shifted from the perception of the wronged, the hard done by, from "I have been sexually abused" to "Thanks, God, for the experience."

I inhaled the spiritual warrior and the divine earthly woman. I disciplined the thoughts to only exist in love. In the silence of accepting that I was alone I realized that I was not alone, and I met my best friend—my soul.

Miracles

The miracle of self-transformation is allowing your heart to open, to surrender and for peace to pour forth. I have found myself, beyond deep wounds and programming, to be a person of unconditional love. This love comes from within me and shows me that this love is who I *truly* am. My life is a true love story. From what I have experienced I can tell you that if you live without love in your life—true, nurturing self-love—then you must pursue this love through self-transformation.

When you experience this love, you will see that self-transformation is the most captivating experience you will ever have. If I had to name the biggest miracle in my life, it would definitely be that through seeking self-transformation I know that *I love myself.*

True Love of the True Woman

My truest love story is that of falling deeply in love with myself. In the sacred ceremony of this experience I am able to experience deep love in my life with my partner and children. I no longer live in fear of keeping a partner or attracting love. I am love, and all those around me receive and are nurtured by this love. When I am in relationships with people today, I pray that in our experience together they will witness their truest aspects and empower their journey through our meeting. I know that seeing this in others is the greatest gift I can give to not only the person receiving the love but also to the entire planet. The more we focus on love, the greater the opportunity for Mother Earth to ascend into her truest, most magnificent expression of nature—free from the pollution of negative thoughts, actions and intentions of the mind. As a woman it is my earthly duty to provide unconditional love to all so that it is reflected back to the true woman, Mother Earth.

Through this process of transformation and connecting wholly with Mother Earth I have witnessed, through my own experience, that we can meet ourselves and become our self-power in any situation, surrounded by any amount of responsibility. Initially our minds will question our ability to transform our lives. Your mind can be seen as a child that knows no better than its conditioning until this child experiences its own inner healing.

Then after this transformation the mind will transform and be the red carpet to your identity of self-power—to your heart, which is the seat of your soul.

So at this point I encourage you that no matter what challenges your life today, win! Love everything you are experiencing. It is teaching you to strive for your ultimate self. Turn everything of yourself, your situation and your relationship with others into an exchange of love. That love may be consciously lived or silently invoked. Silently you may pray or contemplate giving love to another so that they may also seek change and be empowered within their own lives. Remember always that we are each responsible for ourselves. All outside of that is not in our control or related to how we seek change. Always look at a person's behavior and see where it fits with you, and then make the decision that empowers you. Always handle relationships with unconditional love. Fear, hatred, jealousy, anger and greed are definitely not the way to handle others. These associations to others will not empower you, but on many levels of existence they will remove your self-power. Live life having no expectations of how life will be, and you will be prepared with an empowering tool—acceptance.

"Oh Lord, give me the strength to accept what I cannot change."

$\mathcal{B}$ecome Every Breath

What Are Invocations and Why Are They Combined with Conscious Breathing?

In Chapter 3 of this book you will find forty Complete Earthly Woman invocations and the most productive way to use them. The various conscious breathing exercises provided will assist you in overcoming many experiences and subconscious programming mentioned throughout this book. The invocations are the essences of Truth. They will invoke an ancient truth, the female pulse within your heart. Through inhaling each one with conscious breathing you will attune yourself to the vibration of each invocation and the essence of them that exists within your heart.

Working with these invocations and consciously inhaling them is what I have experienced as a powerful healing tool that is constantly available within our own existence. When you do the following invocations you are not taking on something new. You are attuning to your most empowered state of being—the highest level of awareness that already exists within but which you do not always use. Sometimes we struggle through life unaware that such divine assistance is available within us, or we are aware of such assistance, but we are unable to make the connection. We are used to seeking assistance outside of ourselves. The beauty of these invocations is that within your most sacred aspect, your heart, you are the essence of these invocations. Combining this practice with each breath, you will shift the vibration of your physical body, your emotions and your mind to an awakened state of consciousness. Simply by attuning and awakening the sacred female consciousness within your heart.

By practicing what is available here you will invoke and complete an inner transformation within the thinking mind, your behavior programming and your life. Your self-esteem will transform into an abundant river of life. You will blossom into a flowering rose of Truth. I am sure that when you begin using these invocations, you will attune instantly to your female wisdom, which will say, "finally, some wholesome food," as your thoughts at the time of inhaling the invocations will be digesting the divine female consciousness of Mother Earth. These invocations will flood your mind with a river of Truth that will connect to your heart, allowing your life to transform —very easily and very effectively.

As you begin attuning to the invocations you will feel yourself yearning to drink them as the nectar of life as they draw you into their purity. If you surrender to their magnificence and discipline your life to their truth, you will enter your female heart — the heart of Mother Earth. I know through my own transformation and in working with other women and their experiences that these invocations are from the vibration of Mother Earth. I know that she needs women to attune to this divine aspect of themselves. It will both elevate and heal her and elevate and heal humanity. For our precious planet — our most sacred mother — to survive and heal damage that has been done to her, humanity needs to reawaken their most sacred aspect. Humanity needs to begin honoring the sacred female aspect of existence. When this is being accomplished all within existence will be honored.

When we do any self-development work the most effective way to proceed is by including the imagination of the inner child. The child aspect of yourself needs to be a part of the process, or she will stall the process.

Our inner child allows us to awaken. In different cultures they say that our highest consciousness will come into our lives and be activated within our hearts when the inner child is in harmony and gives permission for the experience of an increased level of understanding to take place.

From my personal experience I see the relationship of the inner child as a vital step in merging with your most awakened self. When attuning to your heart through conscious breathing and invocations you are including the participation of the inner child. You are combining the experiences of the inner child and the inner adolescent with the adult through the act of conscious breathing. You are programming all aspects of you within the subconscious mind and on all levels of your existence. This is done by inhaling the Complete Earthly Woman invocations. There is such a magnitude of healing available through the combination of these invocations and conscious breathing, because, as I have already mentioned, these invocations are already part of your most sacred aspect within your heart. You are simply reawakening that expression within yourself. You are focusing on truth, which is the essence of the invocations, and this is allowing you to leave behind the drama within the mind. You will follow virtues and not be confused by the harshness of the material world. When I say material world I refer to living a life unconsciously, where your day consists of living in your mind, your life being dictated by your mind. Where your heart is locked shut, aching for the light of Truth to explode the door so it can inhale a breath of Truth.

There is no denying that when we begin to open the door of the heart, painful memories and experiences will at times appear to us. This will happen either mentally, emotionally or physically. However, there is no need to get caught up in the play of these experiences you witness surfacing. Deal with transformation on a mature level of acceptance by accepting your life, your role and your learning. Cease to let the victim grab hold of you and move beyond. Let go and nurture yourself through your whole transformation with wisdom, not wounds. Embrace what appears to you. Each experience takes you one step closer to your sacred self. Love it. Everything is a calling card for your self-realization. This process is only an action of pure love and simplicity. The only way we can transform wounds is through love—and simplicity. As it is a lack of love that creates wounds.

Inner Silence

Spiritual centering for me is in connecting wholly to inner silence, and it is important to achieve this when mastering self-transformation. When we can sit within this inner silence and it is immediately accessible to us, then we have reached a very elevated step in consciousness. When we master our thoughts, then we are heading straight for this inner silence. Practice looking at every thought and ask if it reflects a positive or a negative intention for your self-transformation. If it reflects a negative, then release it through the awareness that you have seen it and the action of consciously exhaling it from you.

After practicing owning your thoughts so as to locate and

integrate your true personal power, your mind will begin begging to experience inner silence. It will become exhausted with the process of self-transformation and will not want to hear any more. It will come out gasping for air, tired and ready to meet with inner silence. Self-discipline will exhaust the mind into change. Then your transformation will take off and soar like an eagle when the mind steps aside and begins to silently watch and agree that you are a wonderful, loving, vital woman. It will cease to criticize you and cease to trigger thoughts and actions of physical, mental and emotional disharmony. It will learn that when it does this, the heart will immediately pull it in and begin counseling it through words of sacred wisdom.

To invoke this union with the heart, in which it will heal the thought processes of the mind, begin to ask yourself when you are challenged in your self-belief, "What am I healing now? Am I transforming myself for the better?" This is how to turn your negative mind into the positive mind. Take it right back to you. Begin to know that all you see in others is also a part of you. If you do not like what you see, change the situation through changing yourself. You will reclaim your personal power through this transformation, always striving with discipline to move forward. This is the commitment that builds faith and rewards you with an insurmountable inner strength that will be achieved through the abundant flow of courage available within your heart.

We can give away our self-power when we seek protection outside of ourselves. Through failing to control our thoughts and the experiences from these thoughts, we bring into our lives a lack of harmony within the mental and emotional bodies.

In our ability to transform our lives (make all our decisions, participate in our future and our relationships) and in an exchange of self-power, life becomes rewarding, through the act of consciously owning and accepting every aspect of who we are. Accepting what we must change about ourselves, our environment and our relationships. Experiencing yourself in such an honorable way is the precious water that nurtures the budding rose of self-power within your heart. At times, when you begin calling back your self-power, you will see people falling away from you, calling themselves victims of your actions, saying that in finding yourself you are hurting them. When do we really ever have the power to hurt another while simply empowering ourselves if we handle things in an honest, considerate manner? It is our interpretation of who we are and the way that we accept experiences around us that gives us the power to say that another is hurting us. A victim says, "A person hurt me." It is a very healthy process to connect with the victim, to nurture yourself through the acceptance of trauma in your life. However, you must always seek to step beyond conditioning of the ego and falling into the trap of not progressing into self-love. Always seek to move forward from the victim to the path of the spiritual warrior. If you do not like the way another is treating you and if you are old enough to take action, then take it. Thank them for the lesson and move on within your life.

We owe it to ourselves and others as performers in the play of life to continuously seek to improve our lives with values. The tougher the road, the more empowering the change. If your actions have ever intentionally violated, assaulted or betrayed anybody, including yourself, then you must seek to transform yourself and open your heart to truth and love. To forgive yourself through seeking to forgive all. There is no excuse, as there is no road too hard.

A Key Release

A golden droplet of self-realization that we experience in the courage of self-transformation is what I now refer to as a key release—a vital step in the awakening of the Complete Earthly Woman. In trying to explain a *key release* it came to me that the most effective way was through example. Following is my own experience of a key release within my self-transformation.

For the past five years I have experienced radical changes in my weight. I have fluctuated from a size 8 at 116 pounds to a size 18 at 260 pounds with no shift in eating habits or other dramatic lifestyle changes. I had children, but I looked after myself and had terrific births and no complications. Yet my weight continued to balloon in and out. So I began to consciously address this issue. I have tried many solutions—from diets, exercise, creams, body wraps—you name it, I've done it. However, at one point I decided, "This is ridiculous. I am a healthy, motivated, in touch woman, and this weight is symbolic of something, but what?" So I spent time inhaling my invocations and invoking that aspect of myself that is contentedly 116 pounds. After some time and many fluctuations the answer appeared to me. One morning I awoke and my throat was incredibly sore. It almost felt paralyzed. Curiously I wondered what it could be. I am the type of person who rarely runs off to the doctor or claims a cold; I immediately attune to what is behind the physical discomfort. I spent a whole day with this sore throat, and by the end of the day I could barely speak.

In the evening before going to bed I wrote to my heart, something that I do often. I asked my heart to reveal what was behind this sore throat. Why was I experiencing such pain? During the night I awoke to feed our son, and as I was walking through the kitchen I said to myself, "Some custard would be soothing on this throat." As I said this, I suddenly experienced a profound realization.

When I was six years old I became very ill with inflamed tonsils. For weeks I lay in bed only able to eat custard through the teat of a baby's bottle. Eventually I went into the hospital to have my tonsils removed. The whole experience distressed me intensely. Three weeks after having them removed I had ballooned out in weight and was 42 pounds heavier than when I went into the hospital. Since that very point in my life I have had a weight problem.

When realizing this during the night I sat quietly with myself. I heard my inner child speaking to me. She told me she had been afraid. The experience of being asleep during the operation had sent her into shock because of the previous sexual abuse. Part of her withdrew through fear during that operation. The weight was her protection mechanism and her symbol and cry out for losing her personal power. It had already been removed mainly from the act of sexual abuse and this experience had completed the cycle for the child losing her personal will. So in silence we sat together and I nursed her within my heart. I embraced her fear and aligned her to Truth. I told her silently within of her new life as a woman. I encouraged her to want to live as a woman. Then I inhaled that true, empowering, nurturing essence of being a woman, and I exhaled her fear, her misinterpretations and her separateness from today. As I exhaled, I removed a key release.

To experience a key release you address an issue over a period of time, spending time invoking a higher consciousness within you to reflect the lower consciousness of your issue.

Finally a realization occurs within you and you peace together the puzzle. Through inhaling your invocations you will eventually exhale your key release. The invocations I used to trigger this release are included in the invocation groups titled Physical Balance and Peace with your Past in Chapter 3.

The day that you experience a key release you will feel your most empowered aspect explode within your heart. The victory song will sing to you within your mind. Believe me, this is a day to strive for. When seeking a key release do not look at all of your physical issues as physical problems, your emotional issues as emotional problems or your mental issues as mental problems. Look at them as energy that needs reorganizing. Energy that is awaiting to empower your life. In addition, when you seek change within yourself, seek to change into your most empowered self. For example, when I wanted to lose weight I asked to lose weight so I would reflect my inner beauty and for no other reason. I want to live as my best spiritual weight. Seek change to empower the heart, not the mind, and you will achieve overwhelming results.

As my weight continues to fluctuate I know that each realization and key release takes me one step closer to physical-spiritual union. I accept this challenge as my penance. This is what we all strive for. Each one of us has a union to form and each one of us will be challenged either physically, mentally or emotionally when seeking spiritual union. The key, how-ever, is courage and self-love. There have been times when I have experienced moments in my life where I feel I have conquered all of what I felt driven to change. Then as quickly as I experienced living empowered from change, I quickly moved into transforming another issue. This is what I experi-ence with my weight. Mentally or emotionally I am rarely challenged. I feel very spiritually centered in these areas. At times when my body will fluctuate my spiritual energy will fluctuate. After much contemplation I have accepted that my body and the transformation of this body is like an onion and each layer presents itself differently. So what I am saying is that each key release will take you one step closer into spiritual union with what you transcend mentally, emotionally or physically. A key release being just that—another turn within the lock of the sacred heart.

Invoke Your Transformation Within the Heart

Choosing your invocations is the first step in preparing to begin your transformation. The most effective way to do this is to read through all of the invocations from the beginning.

When reading the invocations, try not to read them like you would the newspaper. Ask yourself as you are reading them, "Is this me? Am I living this way or awakening this sacred aspect of the woman in my life?" As you hear your reply, connect with the feeling coming from the invocation. Do you feel this way about yourself, or are you aching to feel this way about yourself? Begin with the invocations that stir the most reaction, choosing one group of seven to work with at one time.

In the following chapter, Transforming Sexuality, is the first group of seven invocations which I began working with, using them to purify the mind and cleanse the cellular memory based on experiences of sexual trauma. It is important to write down any reactions you may have when practicing your invocations. Speak to your heart and ask for assistance to cleanse and purify programming on all levels. By writing down your experiences you will see which emotions, experiences and interpretations created your reactions when aligning to a quality of the Complete Earthly Woman. This mental education and assimilation will further empower the self-transformation within your heart, because the mind will understand what you are doing. It will see results in your recording, and it will therefore join with your heart and allow your heart to educate it along the path of self-transformation.

While you release these aspects of yourself during your sitting you will have placed into the subconscious mind the following instruction and behavior: *Each time you inhale, invoke your most empowered self and the divine healing truth using the invocation you have chosen. Each time you exhale, release the resistances within your mind.*

When you have experiences that affect you in a negative way, picture your invocations and begin to breathe the same way you do when invoking your inner Truth, the Complete Earthly Woman. Doing this will align the situation you are experiencing as well as align you to your most empowered self, the heart.

It is important to know that at the moment you identify with a negative aspect of yourself it is your responsibility to discipline yourself for positive change within. This is where the mind can let itself down. It refuses to believe in itself—in you. It will challenge you. Just know that if you begin to let yourself down, it is your mind resisting the change. Even if the resistance presents itself as physical discomfort, or mental and emotional imbalance, have the courage and belief that you are going to succeed. All you need to do is to connect with your subconscious through breathing. It is very, very simple. Some people say, "How do I believe in myself when my mind will not let me, because it refuses to believe in who I am?"

This is a challenge that can be won. The way to handle this mind is to imagine it as a small child—a child who likes routine in the way of thought patterns and is not aware that it is possible or even necessary to change. The mind does not know life outside of what it experiences, has been or remembers, so change can seem unobtainable and unnecessary. Therefore both encouraging and educating the mind is necessary.

Encouraging Your Inner Child

The next aspect of yourself that needs encouragement to change is your inner child. This can be initiated simply through the following visualization.

Create a picture of your child within; see her face confused in the process of change. Smile at her, pick her up and place her in a car seat in the back of a car. Pat her reassuringly and close the door. See yourself as your most empowered self, getting into the front seat of the car and starting the engine.

In this visualization the child is your childhood, the car is the physical body, the empowered self is your soul and the road your journey. Explain at this point to your child that she can now sit comfortably and enjoy an educating, abundant life filled with love. She is safe. Sitting comforted and guided by the soul, she can live an insightful life of knowing and higher understanding.

This for me is an incredibly effective visualization for realigning to the empowered self. It is effective because the aspect that seeks change is now educating the aspect that innocently sabotages change.

Using Your Invocations in Simple Terms

Choose your group of seven invocations, a group that you feel relates to a specific issue or issues you wish to change in your life.

Spend time whenever you can (preferably daily) to practice invoking each invocation with conscious breathing.

Practice each group until you experience your key release, then move onto the next group.

It's that simple. It is meant to be simple, because in our most empowered center of existence is a radiant life of love and divine simplicity. So move into it. Cease to waste a breath. Direct each breath to the betterment and love of you.

On the following page is an example of the process of consciously inhaling the sacred invocation titled Beauty to further explain how you proceed.

BEAUTY

INVOKE: *I am a beautiful woman*

inhale	I am a beautiful woman
exhale	**I exhale all resistance**
inhale	The beauty of being a woman
exhale	**I exhale all resistance**
inhale	Is all that I am
exhale	**I exhale all resistance**
inhale	Daughter
exhale	**I exhale all resistance**
inhale	Girl
exhale	**I exhale all resistance**
inhale	Sister
exhale	**I exhale all resistance**
inhale	Friend
exhale	**I exhale all resistance**
inhale	Mother
exhale	**I exhale all resistance**
inhale	I am the divine expression of love
exhale	**I exhale all resistance**
inhale	As in every aspect
exhale	**I exhale all resistance**
inhale	I am a woman

Sacred Invocations of
the Complete Earthly Woman

Complete Earthly Woman – Invocations

Provided here are the seven groups of invocations that you can freely choose from. Select any group that appeals to you and aligns you to the issues you wish to transform. You can refer to the previous chapter for an explanation on how to use them effectively. Have fun with these invocations and know that they are sacred values from the womb of Mother Earth. In practicing these invocations you will take yourself far along the path of self-transformation and align yourself to the magnificence of the Complete Earthly Woman.

I suggest to you that at any time combine any of the invocations provided to create your own personalized group of invocations to practice. The invocation groups outlined here are what I use to work with others and myself. You may at some point be drawn to specific invocations and feel that it would be more beneficial for you to practice them. This is wonderful, it is the aspect within you calling out for you to take a direction within yourself, openly let it happen.

To practice each group of invocations, begin by sitting quietly, deeply inhaling and exhaling. Repeat to yourself within your mind that you are moving into each experience you wish to release. Begin to pay attention to the pictures and discussions that present themselves within your mind. See different experiences and be consciously aware to exhale them. With each exhale tell yourself you are letting go. As you exhale, breathe out all pictures, feelings and emotions that present themselves to you. There is no need to get caught up in the emotions; just keep breathing and keep letting go. It is more difficult to hang on than it is to let go.

As you exhale look to the first line of your invocation. Inhale the first line as you read it to yourself. Exhale your discomforts and resistance. You may close your eyes as you exhale and reopen them when you read the invocation for the inhale. (To see this refer to the Beauty invocation on page 38.)

Remember that this process is simplicity. Invoking inner Truth with each breath. Find your own rhythm to identify with—the aspects you wish to purify.

Grouped Invocations of the Complete Earthly Woman

Transforming Sexuality		*Peace with Your Past*	
Loyal	*page* 47	Expectation	*page* 48
Sensual	46	Wise	49
Womb of Life	44	Happiness	52
One with Mother Earth	45	Mother	54
Accepting	50	Father	55
Lover	53	Realistic	59
Nurturing	58	Precious	62

Sacred Invocations of the Complete Earthly Woman

The above are patterns of invocations proven to give results. Feel inspired to move further within yourself through creating your own group of invocations as previously mentioned; all patterns can give results.

Over the days after you have practiced your invocations you will become aware that at different times throughout the day your invocations will appear in your mind. When this happens begin to breathe exactly as you do when you practice them. Inhaling what you remember of the invocations you have practiced. Doing this will invoke a peaceful calm state within yourself, through breathing in a controlled rhythm. At times spontaneous breathing will happen. At this time consciously exhale all resistance to the experience. Exhale the thoughts that appear in your mind. Exhale all resistance to change and all fear and disbelief that you have, and continue to change. Eventually you will experience spontaneous calm breathing and cease having to control your breathing to invoke a state of peace and self-realization.

BEAUTY

INVOKE: *I am a beautiful woman*

inhale	The beauty of being a woman	exhale
inhale	Is all that I am	exhale
inhale	Daughter	exhale
inhale	Girl	exhale
inhale	Sister	exhale
inhale	Friend	exhale
inhale	Mother	exhale
inhale	I am the divine expression of love	exhale
inhale	As in every aspect	exhale
inhale	I am a woman	exhale

TRUTH

INVOKE: *I am divine female truth*

inhale	Truth is the light within my heart	exhale
inhale	That radiates the glow	exhale
inhale	Of inner wisdom	exhale
inhale	Purity and the strength to be me	exhale

UNCONDITIONAL LOVE
INVOKE: *I am unconditional love*

inhale	As a woman	*exhale*
inhale	I am a divine instrument	*exhale*
inhale	Of unconditional love	*exhale*
inhale	May this love	*exhale*
inhale	Shine as a temple of light	*exhale*
inhale	Shine within all	*exhale*
inhale	As I freely give love	*exhale*

WOMB OF LIFE
INVOKE: *I am the womb of life*

inhale	With each breath that I take	*exhale*
inhale	I merge within the womb of life	*exhale*
inhale	That which I connect	*exhale*
inhale	That which I came	*exhale*
inhale	That which I am	*exhale*

DUTY TO HUMANITY
INVOKE: *I am service to humanity*

inhale	As a woman my duty to humanity	*exhale*
inhale	Is to heal every aspect of who I am	*exhale*
inhale	In this moment	*exhale*
inhale	To connect within my heart	*exhale*
inhale	In this connection I freely	*exhale*
inhale	Give to humanity	*exhale*
inhale	Clarity, compassion, truth	*exhale*
inhale	Pure unconditional love	*exhale*
inhale	It is in the beauty of creating new life	*exhale*
inhale	As a woman	*exhale*
inhale	That I shape humanity	*exhale*
inhale	Through the abundant values of love	*exhale*
inhale	Love which I give my children	*exhale*
inhale	Our children	*exhale*

ONE WITH MOTHER EARTH
INVOKE: *I am one with Mother Earth*

inhale	I am one with Mother Earth	*exhale*
inhale	As her heartbeat	*exhale*
inhale	Her gift of new life	*exhale*
inhale	Resides within me	*exhale*
inhale	We are one	*exhale*

ENCOURAGING

INVOKE: *I give encouragement*

inhale	As a woman I am encouraging	*exhale*
inhale	I give encouragement freely	*exhale*
inhale	May all develop in the light	*exhale*
inhale	Unconditional love	*exhale*
inhale	Of self-confidence	*exhale*

SENSUAL

INVOKE: *I am sensual female purity*

inhale	This body is the temple of purity	*exhale*
inhale	Skin so fine	*exhale*
inhale	Hands so gentle	*exhale*
inhale	Lips so tender	*exhale*
inhale	Hair so soft	*exhale*
inhale	I hear music within my heart	*exhale*
inhale	As I feel golden hands of tenderness	*exhale*
inhale	Stroke my body	*exhale*
inhale	I am safe within	*exhale*
inhale	Sensuality and purity	*exhale*
inhale	That of a woman	*exhale*
inhale	I protect this sensuality	*exhale*
inhale	In the acceptance of truth	*exhale*
inhale	And the boundaries of values	*exhale*

FAITHFUL
INVOKE: ***I am a faithful woman***

inhale	As a woman I am faithful	*exhale*
inhale	In doing so	*exhale*
inhale	I am nurturing to all	*exhale*
inhale	Every situation or experience	*exhale*

LOYAL
INVOKE: ***I am loyal***

inhale	As a woman I embrace loyalty	*exhale*
inhale	As loyalty given	*exhale*
inhale	Will give nectar to the flower	*exhale*
inhale	Within the heart	*exhale*

RELIABLE
INVOKE: ***I am reliable***

inhale	As a woman I give stability	*exhale*
inhale	Within all relationships	*exhale*
inhale	Through being reliable	*exhale*
inhale	And forthright	*exhale*

COMPANION

INVOKE: *I am a true companion*

inhale	A true companion is a woman	exhale
inhale	Of unconditional love	exhale
inhale	Offering the stability of a rock	exhale
inhale	That which will never wash away	exhale
inhale	In the currents of life	exhale
inhale	A true companion am I	exhale

EXPECTATION

INVOKE: *I have no expectation*

inhale	As a woman I have no expectation	exhale
inhale	Of others or myself	exhale
inhale	Just pure delight in who I am today	exhale
inhale	All I have to give	exhale
inhale	I seek change within who I am	exhale
inhale	With no expectations	exhale
inhale	In the behavior of others	exhale
inhale	Or the outcome of situations	exhale
inhale	I am delighted by me	exhale
inhale	By all	exhale

INTUITIVE
INVOKE: *My key is my intuition*

inhale	As a woman I am the	*exhale*
inhale	Heartbeat of Mother Earth	*exhale*
inhale	I flow in the river of light within	*exhale*
inhale	My thoughts and actions	*exhale*
inhale	Are guided by this river	*exhale*
inhale	This river of intuition	*exhale*
inhale	Is the golden voice of the	*exhale*
inhale	Heart	*exhale*

WISE
INVOKE: *I am pure wisdom*

inhale	The ancient wisdom	*exhale*
inhale	Of the ancient woman	*exhale*
inhale	Unfolds within	*exhale*
inhale	In love, kindness and service	*exhale*
inhale	I give this wisdom	*exhale*
inhale	Golden words	*exhale*
inhale	Golden actions	*exhale*
inhale	All to the flow of humanity	*exhale*

ACCEPTING
INVOKE: *I am accepting always*

inhale	I am accepting of all situations	*exhale*
inhale	Of all	*exhale*
inhale	Who come, go and stay	*exhale*
inhale	In my life	*exhale*
inhale	Their lives are truth to them	*exhale*
inhale	As mine is truth to me	*exhale*
inhale	The most gracious love I can give	*exhale*
inhale	To others and myself	*exhale*
inhale	Is the acceptance	*exhale*
inhale	That all	*exhale*
inhale	Is perfect	*exhale*

PEACEFUL
INVOKE: *I am peaceful*

inhale	In peace	*exhale*
inhale	I can truly empower	*exhale*
inhale	The gifts	*exhale*
inhale	The beauty	*exhale*
inhale	In being a woman	*exhale*
inhale	In peace	*exhale*
inhale	I can truly	*exhale*
inhale	Become one with Mother Earth	*exhale*

EXCITED
INVOKE: *Life excites me*

inhale	I am excited for life	*exhale*
inhale	To continue every day	*exhale*
inhale	To discover and wholly become	*exhale*
inhale	All of the beauty that exists	*exhale*
inhale	Within my heart	*exhale*
inhale	I am excited by my challenges	*exhale*
inhale	By my relationships	*exhale*
inhale	I am excited by life	*exhale*
inhale	The changes I make	*exhale*
inhale	To merge within the harmony	*exhale*
inhale	Of being a woman	*exhale*
inhale	As nothing is ever difficult	*exhale*
inhale	Only rewarding	*exhale*

SAD
INVOKE: *I move forward from sadness*

inhale	Sadness is the expression of change	*exhale*
inhale	It is the expression of acceptance	*exhale*
inhale	As in transforming sadness	*exhale*
inhale	Into happiness	*exhale*
inhale	I accept to change	*exhale*
inhale	Sadness is an equal gift to happiness	*exhale*
inhale	It rewards me with	*exhale*
inhale	Self-awareness	*exhale*

HAPPINESS
INVOKE: *I am happiness — I am joy*

inhale	In experiencing happiness as a woman	*exhale*
inhale	I give others joy	*exhale*
inhale	I give freely from the place	*exhale*
inhale	Of divine purity	*exhale*
inhale	My Heart	*exhale*

EMOTIONAL
INVOKE: *I am the master of my emotions*

inhale	As a woman I master my emotions	*exhale*
inhale	So as not to imbalance my thoughts	*exhale*
inhale	So as not to create disharmony	*exhale*
inhale	In my inner peace	*exhale*
inhale	Or the inner peace of others	*exhale*

LOVER

INVOKE: *I am a lover within my heart comfortable in my inner boundaries*

inhale	To be a lover of a woman	*exhale*
inhale	Is to be the lover of Mother Earth	*exhale*
inhale	Self-awareness of being a woman	*exhale*
inhale	Is a jewel which I place	*exhale*
inhale	In a union of love	*exhale*
inhale	With a chosen soul	*exhale*
inhale	To be a lover, my lover	*exhale*
inhale	Is a gift	*exhale*
inhale	A gift that is protected	*exhale*
inhale	In respect, trust and honor	*exhale*
inhale	As I honor my gift	*exhale*
inhale	In being a	*exhale*
inhale	Gentle nurturing caressing lover	*exhale*
inhale	The choices that I make	*exhale*
inhale	To share my inner beauty	*exhale*
inhale	In this way	*exhale*
inhale	Is a gift of love to me	*exhale*
inhale	And my beloved in which I share	*exhale*

MOTHER

INVOKE: *Mother is love*

inhale	A golden key in the rhythm	*exhale*
inhale	Of being a mother	*exhale*
inhale	Is to be a mother of right action	*exhale*
inhale	Of integrity, love, kindness and purity	*exhale*
inhale	As a healer of humanity	*exhale*
inhale	It is the pure beauty given to the child	*exhale*
inhale	The wholeness to the woman	*exhale*
inhale	As being a mother	*exhale*
inhale	A true mother	*exhale*
inhale	Takes the girl	*exhale*
inhale	The daughter	*exhale*
inhale	The sister	*exhale*
inhale	To the center of the female heart	*exhale*
inhale	Into the vibration of re-creation	*exhale*
inhale	The golden gift and oneness	*exhale*
inhale	With Mother Earth	*exhale*
inhale	I surrender in love to being a mother	*exhale*
inhale	I give love to my mother	*exhale*

FATHER
INVOKE: *I honor my father*

inhale	A father is a man of sacred wisdom	*exhale*
inhale	Who is a teacher through his actions	*exhale*
inhale	With unconditional love	*exhale*
inhale	I thank my father	*exhale*
inhale	As who he is	*exhale*
inhale	Gives me who I am	*exhale*
inhale	For as a daughter to this sacred man	*exhale*
inhale	I am a gift	*exhale*
inhale	A gift of self-realization	*exhale*
inhale	A gift of life	*exhale*
inhale	He is a true teacher	*exhale*
inhale	Companion and inspiration	*exhale*
inhale	He is a key to finding my True self	*exhale*
inhale	I thank and honor my father	*exhale*
inhale	May he thank and honor me	*exhale*

CONSCIENTIOUS
INVOKE: *I am conscientious of truth*

inhale	To be conscientious is to shine	*exhale*
inhale	As a woman, a light of inner wisdom	*exhale*
inhale	To be humbly accepted	*exhale*
inhale	In the eyes of others	*exhale*
inhale	As this female strength is a gift to all	*exhale*
inhale	To be conscientious is	*exhale*
inhale	Action of feminine grace	*exhale*

PASSIONATE
INVOKE: *I am passionate*

inhale	In the act of being passionate	*exhale*
inhale	I excite others	*exhale*
inhale	As a passionate woman	*exhale*
inhale	I give joy from the depth	*exhale*
inhale	Of my feminine creative light	*exhale*
inhale	In the act of being passionate	*exhale*
inhale	I am innocent and empowering	*exhale*

FORGIVING
INVOKE: *I am forgiving*

inhale	As a woman	*exhale*
inhale	Forgiveness is all that I am	*exhale*
inhale	Unconditional love	*exhale*
inhale	Forgiveness	*exhale*

KNOWING
INVOKE: *I am knowing*

inhale	My inner knowing	*exhale*
inhale	Shines like a beacon of Truth	*exhale*
inhale	In all of my choices, actions	*exhale*
inhale	Decisions and thoughts	*exhale*
inhale	It is the inner knowing	*exhale*
inhale	Of Mother Earth	*exhale*
inhale	The voice of the mother	*exhale*

FRIEND
INVOKE: *I am a true friend*

inhale	As a woman	*exhale*
inhale	I am a best friend	*exhale*
inhale	A friend of truth and kindness	*exhale*
inhale	A friend sharing life	*exhale*
inhale	A friend not always of words	*exhale*
inhale	Or physical togetherness	*exhale*
inhale	But constantly of the heart	*exhale*
inhale	Friendship I give openly	*exhale*
inhale	To those of truth	*exhale*
inhale	As the gift of my friendship sits within	*exhale*
inhale	A golden box within my heart	*exhale*
inhale	That will open freely	*exhale*
inhale	In the exchange of kindness	*exhale*

SUPPORTIVE
INVOKE: *I am a supportive woman*

inhale	I live my female connection	*exhale*
inhale	To Mother Earth	*exhale*
inhale	I give all support of divine wisdom	*exhale*
inhale	Guidance and unconditional love	*exhale*
inhale	As in my actions of being	*exhale*
inhale	Supportive to others	*exhale*
inhale	I support that which I know I am	*exhale*
inhale	LOVE	*exhale*

MY MALE

INVOKE: *I am centered yin and yang—balanced*

inhale	In being a woman of harmony	exhale
inhale	I balance my male aspect within	exhale
inhale	My truest relationship is that of myself	exhale
inhale	For I am a man and woman	exhale
inhale	That merge as one	exhale
inhale	In the dance of wholeness	exhale
inhale	Around the sacred fire of truth	exhale
inhale	Within my heart	exhale
inhale	I appreciate my male side	exhale
inhale	As he empowers my female side	exhale
inhale	And the truth that I am a woman	exhale

NURTURING

INVOKE: *To nurture others is to nurture me*

inhale	To be nurtured as a woman	exhale
inhale	Is to be nurturing to all	exhale
inhale	It is to connect with truth	exhale
inhale	Mother Earth	exhale
inhale	Knowing that as a woman we are one	exhale
inhale	One with the womb of the mother	exhale
inhale	That the delight in being nurtured	exhale
inhale	Is the delight in nurturing others	exhale

CREATIVE
INVOKE: *My creativity is who I am*

inhale	To be creative as a woman	*exhale*
inhale	Is to color the world	*exhale*
inhale	It is to fill hearts with warmth	*exhale*
inhale	Oneness, joy and rhythm	*exhale*
inhale	It is to inspire the heartbeat	*exhale*
inhale	Of our planet's souls	*exhale*
inhale	Our children	*exhale*

REALISTIC
INVOKE: *I am always realistic*

inhale	The realism with being a true woman	*exhale*
inhale	Is a gift of being in harmony	*exhale*
inhale	With the feminine rhythm	*exhale*
inhale	The beauty of the earth	*exhale*
inhale	As to be realistic	*exhale*
inhale	Is the golden connection	*exhale*
inhale	To being the light of truth	*exhale*

DAUGHTER

INVOKE: *I love being a daughter*

inhale	To be a daughter is a gift	*exhale*
inhale	It is the beginning of life	*exhale*
inhale	The role in which	*exhale*
inhale	I become a woman	*exhale*
inhale	It is the identity of my inner child	*exhale*
inhale	The experience of my life	*exhale*
inhale	That bridges my heart	*exhale*
inhale	To the gift and right action	*exhale*
inhale	Of acceptance	*exhale*
inhale	That I accept	*exhale*
inhale	Who I am	*exhale*
inhale	What I have become	*exhale*
inhale	Who I am becoming	*exhale*
inhale	I accept my parents	*exhale*
inhale	For sharing their lives	*exhale*
inhale	For their love	*exhale*
inhale	In this acceptance	*exhale*
inhale	I love me	*exhale*
inhale	Who I am	*exhale*
inhale	And the gift that I have given	*exhale*
inhale	To those souls	*exhale*
inhale	That I am the daughter	*exhale*

SISTER

INVOKE: *I love being a sister*

inhale	A sister is a true companion	*exhale*
inhale	A companion of laughter	*exhale*
inhale	Joy and unconditional love	*exhale*
inhale	To be a sister	*exhale*
inhale	Is to give a friendship	*exhale*
inhale	Of loyalty, trust and oneness	*exhale*
inhale	To be a sister	*exhale*
inhale	Is female companionship	*exhale*
inhale	Free from judgment	*exhale*
inhale	And expectation	*exhale*
inhale	To be a sister is the gift	*exhale*
inhale	Of giving and receiving	*exhale*
inhale	In giving love, trust and joy	*exhale*
inhale	In nurturing my brother/sister	*exhale*
inhale	I am blessed to have giggled	*exhale*
inhale	And held hands as a child	*exhale*
inhale	With true companionship	*exhale*
inhale	As in being a sister	*exhale*
inhale	I have become the purity	*exhale*
inhale	Of sharing life and love	*exhale*

GRANDMOTHER
INVOKE: *I love being a grandmother/mother/me*

inhale	A sacred gift of being a woman	*exhale*
inhale	Is the flowering	*exhale*
inhale	Of being a grandmother	*exhale*
inhale	A grandmother	*exhale*
inhale	Is the combination of wisdom	*exhale*
inhale	And service to the family	*exhale*
inhale	Through the right action	*exhale*
inhale	Of being a mother of peace	*exhale*
inhale	Through the selfless joy	*exhale*
inhale	Of giving love	*exhale*

PRECIOUS
INVOKE: *I am a precious woman*

inhale	A woman is a precious gift	*exhale*
inhale	To be protected	*exhale*
inhale	As the most sacred	*exhale*
inhale	Golden light of love	*exhale*
inhale	I am this precious light	*exhale*
inhale	I hold myself in my own arms	*exhale*
inhale	In love with that which I am	*exhale*
inhale	A woman	*exhale*
inhale	I give myself to each person	*exhale*
inhale	Each relationship	*exhale*
inhale	Only where I am nurtured	*exhale*
inhale	As this precious gift	*exhale*

POSITIVE
INVOKE: *I am always positive*

inhale	To be a woman	*exhale*
inhale	Is to be the essence of positive love	*exhale*
inhale	To shine this love upon all	*exhale*
inhale	And within	*exhale*
inhale	To be unwavering	*exhale*
inhale	To bring all into the light of positivity	*exhale*
inhale	I am a woman of harmony	*exhale*
inhale	A positive woman	*exhale*
inhale	Therefore a sacred teacher	*exhale*

Seek to Move Within

No Longer a Victim

Allowing the victim of your life to run your life and to continue to create your experiences is pollution. It will break down your natural life force energy and create disharmony within your evolution. When you put yourself on the "breathe easy" program within this book you will dissolve the pollution so you can inhale clarity into your every moment. An empowering healing technique that I have experienced is to access your connection to the earth within your womb and her wisdom through your heart. This is easily done through conscious breathing. So by breathing into the consciousness that is the essence of the earth, we are able to transmute all negative programming and access the center of ourselves—our heart.

I truly believe that the invocations provided throughout this book have been given from the spirit of Mother Earth. They are a sacred list of virtues from the womb of the earth. Through conscious breathing and the attunement to these sacred invocations, we are able to align all parts of ourselves, such as our mind, our physical body and our emotions, to the wisdom and purity of the soul. We do this by simply learning to inhale into our female virtues, which are stored as sacred scribes within the female womb as within the womb of our sacred Mother Earth.

Throughout this book I tell a common story of abuse, violation and betrayal—three words that can sound so dramatic and difficult to heal.

Yet are they? Not really, when you consider that these three words—when experienced as divine action within your life—have the capacity to take you into the most beautiful aspect of yourself you could ever wish to find. Accepting these experiences and their consequences will open the door of light within, and you will be forever guided by the wisdom of the soul.

The Initial Shift

When I began seeking change within myself I was living what seemed to be a mundane existence. There was no spark in my life. I had a physical relationship with a special person, yet there was no love. In all ways my life was an expression of this lack of love.

I projected within my mental, emotional and physical framework, "Stay away. I do not have the capacity to love you." I had been desperately seeking a permanent relationship to show myself that I could be loved, that I was worthy of love. I hoped that in giving love to another I would be loved. Instead I found that I could not love. The other person's lack of love toward me showed me both my lack of love to others and myself.

When I was first prompted to change aspects of myself, I was afraid. Initially I was completely ignorant of the benefits of spiritual practices and of consciously connecting with the earth and the soul. When I made the first connection in which I felt my soul filling my heart, I was overcome with companionship and worthiness.

All within me worked together until I wholly accepted the divine radiance within my heart—the golden voice of my intuition. The most nurturing and fulfilling experience of my life has been becoming acquainted with this sacred voice—the voice of the Complete Earthly Woman. Since knowing of her beauty, I strive to embody her glowing radiance, like that of the sun. I seek to exist within as her grace, the grace of the most pure swan, walking through life in rhythm with the most ancient earthly drumbeat, the essence of earthly self-esteem. Her grace is the inner connection to sacred wisdom, her radiance, the radiance of Truth. Exist as a conscious connection to the womb of Mother Earth, fully integrating as a complete, whole, loving person, knowing that to become this inner beauty it is imperative to be aware of our spiritual heritage and the spiritual duties of being a woman.

Cease to be Afraid

Knowing now of the inner beauty awaiting, do you fear the changes that will come when empowering your True self? Perhaps all you seek you are afraid to be. Most times we are lost because of our interpretation of emotional pain. If this is so, then here is the opportunity to interpret life differently, in a positive, self-empowered level of understanding.

If at any time in your life you feel lost, then ask yourself, "When I'm lost, who's looking after me and truly nurturing me?" Well, not you, because you're lost. You don't know which actions come from your True self or which come from your fearful self. If this is the case, then who are you? If you don't know who or where you are, then you are not living as your

True self within. You are living as your fearful self without. Without the relationship of complete, self-empowering love.

This love I speak of is the connection to loving yourself. When we love ourselves we are never lost, because we are empowered to own all of who we are. Most times we are lost because we do not want to own all of who we are and the experiences we have had. We are living fear, confusion or pain, but this is perfectly all right. There have been times in my life when I have been so lost that I thought I had checked out of the planet. I was nowhere to be found. My life was an assortment of confusion and pain.

I was living without self-love and was not even aware that self-love was a quality we were meant to have. Self-esteem was a word with no meaning. I only realized self-esteem when it awoke from within. After I had removed a great deal of interpretations and grief that had controlled my adult life. My inner child and adolescent had projected their acute sadness and grief into my life. My inner child hid within layers of body weight. My adolescent begged to leave the body through different forms of drug abuse, refusing to face what was inside. In no way can I blame them. But as an adult it was my responsibility to heal their pain and remove their grief.

There have been times when, while identifying with my issues, I did not know what I was facing—both mentally and emotionally. Yet during each experience of purification I felt driven to get to the end of the process. My heart somehow blocked my mind from judging my issues and allowed me to heal them. This action of the mind is what I affectionately call "spiritual amnesia." This is where you are invoked to make changes courageously and painlessly — changes you would not normally make. Where you absolutely know that your action of change is the right action and you are driven by faith.

If you are concerned for your self-transformation because you struggle with discipline and the ability to face challenges, look within. It is probably your inner child wanting to hide, confused at the steps you take, and your adolescent avoiding self-responsibility, possibly due to fear of failure. An adolescent with self-worth issues will step away from responsibility rather than risk failure.

Nurturing these two aspects of yourself is simple. Know that they are part of you and that they do not always want to jump into your adult life and assist you in moving forward. They have created their own interpretations of your life. You need to accept that their interpretation is all they know your life to be. As an adult I gave up a marijuana addiction that kept me in denial of my life. I began smoking as an adolescent, and my adolescent self said that life as an adult had to include smoking, otherwise there would be no life. She demonstrated this through seven suicide attempts. She needed the denial.

To create a new life and empower my adult self I had to open my heart—after accepting the pain of the inner child and the adolescent.

Today I understand my life differently. I experience my inner child and adolescent differently. Living as an adult within my heart I see them as an inner child and her experiences and an adolescent and her experiences. The adult is my heart, and my heart is filtering and guiding both my inner child and adolescent. They move within my heart, becoming free from any bondage of misguided interpretations, experiences or grief.

How Am I Hiding My Issues?

Two protection strategies that I had to filter through the heart were the drug addiction of my adolescent and the obesity of my inner child. The severe weight gain that occurred when I was seven years old was a strategy that said, "Stay away, I am unattractive. Look the other way." It was a protection from sexual abuse. My drug addiction said, "I am weak. I am easily led, easily distracted and am convincing myself that I am comfortable in my life. I am just having a good time. I know how to party. I don't want to know what's outside my front door, so better to look through rose-colored glasses." These glasses had taken me in and out of each day without a thought about who I was, what was expected of me or what I was becoming. I did not have to face the insecurity within my life or my relationships. I did not have to think about my family or expectations I might have had regarding their behavior toward me.

By loving and appreciating my inner child and adolescent I create my whole woman within. Humbly and happily I accept their contribution to this life as they have created my adult life by coping under extraordinary circumstances. I love them. As a woman, as a mother and as a partner, I love all of myself. I nurture every aspect of myself by accepting that I would be fantasizing if I thought my life should have made different turns. I know that I have done well, for the simple reason that I wanted to change my life. I wanted to feel and become radiant, glowing, self-abundant worthiness. Just as you do. This is why you are reading this book. There must be some action in your life—either from the present or the past —which you want to accept. Some experience that says, "Embrace this and pass through this to divine, pure self-love." To where you only seek love within, and when you find this love within you, it will attract love throughout all aspects of your life. Exciting, don't you think? It is exciting that we have this capacity to both change and live as an individual of unconditional love. I know that I am excited. My inner child today feels like a princess in self-appreciation. My adolescent is happy to be responsible for right action and the path of Truth. My heart feels safe, empowering and embracing, and living in this sacred heart is everything you can inhale within this book.

Responsibility to Life

In this life you are on a sacred journey; you owe it to who you truly are to be both responsible for this journey and in love with this journey. To be responsible to contribute in right action within the relationship to yourself, others and all aspects of this planet. We already know that the values of civilization fell.

Today, however, you can soar like an eagle. Look around. Make choices. You can either stay stuck in the fear of identifying with all that you have experienced in your life and who you have become as a person, or you can have the courage to look at yourself, accept who you are and rebuild the relationship with your inner self. This can be invoked either through transforming physical experience, mental interpretation, emotional trauma or, at times, participation in a particular behavior—addiction. There are countless ways to transform your life and your way of thinking into a position of self-empowerment.

From my experience, simplicity is the most precise and profound approach to self-transformation. In the action of simplicity we drop judgment and adopt compassion. We move away from confusion and embody knowing. We step forward into transformation and dissolve fear. Simplicity is within your heart. It is your inner conversation within yourself. It is your intuition. It is the aspect of yourself you will trust more and more as you blossom throughout your process. It is the golden voice to which you will become responsible through your actions to both yourself and others.

A Moment of Simplicity

Within your imagination or feelings, connect with a behavior of which you want to let go. Now, in your mind, see yourself participating in this behavior. How do you feel mentally and emotionally when you experience this behavior? When you connect to this behavior, accept that you want to change it. Consciously inhale the will to transform, and exhale the resistance to transform.

Move deeper and deeper into your experience by controlled, connected conscious breathing. Through this act of breathing, a realization will occur. This realization will be the moment that you identify with the cause of this behavior. You will feel or see, even if only slightly, that you have identified with a building block that is part of or the entire aspect of this behavior. At this point of realization you are able to transform. The following is a simple exercise that I suggest for this moment of realization.

In the exact moment of identifying with your behavior, close your eyes. Continue to move deeper into your controlled conscious breathing. Inhale deeply in through your nose and out through your mouth. In your mind, see yourself standing wet in front of the sun. See steam rise up toward the sun off your skin from your whole body, slowly drifting into the light of the sun. As you watch this vapor drift away, consciously inhale this positive invocation: *With each breath I become the divine clarity of this golden light as I let go of this destructive behavior, accepting it as an instrument of sacred teaching.* Inhaling this invocation will empower you to change, and exhaling all resistance will allow you to change.

In breath, connect with the vision of this steam that rises from your skin. This steam is your behavior and the experience that programmed your behavior. With each breath watch the behavior—*steam*—drift away. As you continue to breathe in through your nose and out through your mouth, thank the behavior. Thank it with the knowing that it has been a wonderful teacher and this experience of healing yourself is honored by you as soul growth.

This visualization is simple. It is something that can be done at any time, even while doing other things. If you maintain sure, steady, controlled breathing while connecting to this behavior, you will re-create your behavior, no matter where you are or what your circumstances.

If getting the picture is difficult, focus more on the breath and what you wish to achieve rather than the visualization. The most important part of cleansing the mind is the conscious breathing—the in-breath of the invocation and the out-breath of what you seek to change. This can be described as a form of thought replacement therapy. Identify with a negative thought pattern or action and replace it with a positive one. The only difference is that in this experience you are replacing thoughts and behavior through breathing, and invoking what already exists within through breathing, what you already do every minute of every day.

Oxygen is the life force of the brain—the information center of the mind. When we are practicing conscious breathing and invocations you inhale clarity, purity and intention as part of the life force. The oxygen then purifies the negative thoughts. This is when our use for oxygen becomes empowered through our intention to re-create and co-create within our minds. When the mind through breath connects to the heart. As the heart is the intention and the mind the instrument and vehicle that communicates out intention and empowers our action. Our need for breath allows you to transform even when your mind is busy and bogged down with responsibilities and tasks.

You will also find that the more frequently you connect to the thinking mind through the action of conscious breathing, you will have fewer and fewer experiences of your mind being weighed down with erratic thoughts, behavior and stress. This is because your mind will be focused on the peaceful transformation of your breathing and not on the creation of a million undisciplined thoughts of "what if" and "maybe." My mind was the queen of these types of thoughts. I moved in and out of my own performance, continuously re-creating over and over again the same conflicts to inner truth.

Resistance of the Thinking Mind

At the completion of this visualization it is the appropriate time to discuss resistance from the thinking mind. You may hear this resistance at moments of direct experiences with empowering aspects of yourself. The mind will attempt to sabotage the process of growth. It will begin by saying, "Soul growth, ascending within the heart—what is all of this?" Or maybe it is telling you that you have done this. Check to see if your mind is allowing you to remain in the moment of experiencing the beauty of letting go to your truly empowered self. If it is not leaving you in silence—in beauty—then it is not joining in the union. As frustrating as this can be, this questioning of the mind is a vital behavior not to leave behind. The mind must be the chaperone on the journey of self-transformation.

The mind is your source of communication and the archive of your earthly experiences. I hear people say, "I want to forget the negative aspect of the mind and live in self-love." In my understanding, the negative aspect of the mind must be completely dissolved into love, accomplished through your level of understanding and your interpretations of your life. The clearer the purification of the mind on all levels, the more empowering the self-transformation.

Today it is not as easy to live your life and remain unconscious. The resources to change destructive behavior as the creator of all in your life are here. Therefore, it is your duty to change, your responsibility to your creation.

When you are courageously responsible for yourself, then the self-esteem of the planet can elevate above lower energies such as disease, poverty, violence, self-destruction and betrayal. These lower aspects will dissolve into the purification of society and the planet. Your own inner transformation is a true way that will assist in healing the earth and the destruction of our environment. The destruction of the planet is an easy topic to ignore when you are living in denial of your own pollution and destruction. However, as you transform you will begin to embrace life as unconditional love and a miracle. You will feel Mother Earth making her transformation, and this is when the issues of her health and environmental capacity to heal will become an important aspect of your life. To empower this transformation and connection with this magnificent beauty, Mother Earth, *you must seek to have* this sacred connection with her. Your sacred connection with her will undoubtedly empower your sacred connection within yourself.

Simple Understanding

What is transformational energy? It is energy that creates the experience of self-transformation. It is the energy of our greatest teachers that takes us to the beauty of seeking self-empowerment. It is understanding why and how you are changing. When assimilated correctly, transformational energy will empower personal transformation with logical under-standing. Again, I refer to simplicity. It is the key to unlocking ancient wisdom within your heart. You will know when you are experiencing this ancient wisdom, because you will hear words that invoke the response of, "sounds easy enough" or "that makes sense." Simple understanding.

It is the moment in which you receive answers from the wisdom of your conscious self. It will become easier to remain in the expression of the conscious self when the mind has mastered simple understanding. You can only reach the point of simple understanding through discipline of the mind. Self-discipline. It is the moment in which you will chant to your-self, "With my knowing comes the responsibility for my right action." When we identify with a behavior, thought process or action that disempowers us, it is our responsibility to take action to clear the behavior patterns and move forward until it has been replaced with conscious understanding and unconditional love. Once you have disciplined your self-transformation through belief in yourself, then you will reach the point of simple understanding, which would be seen by some as intuition.

For the purpose of this moment we will refer to intuition as simple understanding, because it will show you to listen for simplicity. This is how to easily identify with your intuition. Love and acceptance are examples of simplicity in action.

The times when you experience this simplicity are the moments in which you have placed your normal thinking mind in the backseat. There it sits, encouraged to enjoy a ride of Soul Truth. In the front seat of your journey is your life's purpose. Divine Truth navigates life's purpose, and together they create your life, which transforms into a celebration of incarnation. When you begin moving through life with this understanding, you will wholly integrate as one and experience the true expression of the heart.

This is the most empowering era upon this planet for the shift of celebrated consciousness into the vibration of the heart. Where is the reason not to go deep within yourself? Have the faith that deep within, you are only an expression of love, in your most empowered existence. Be that love. I know from experience that all you have to do is ask with sincerity, and the universe will provide an abundance of resources for your self-transformation. This is what happened to me.

I have identified today through my own healing and a shift in understanding that the lack of love demonstrated throughout my childhood represented the lack of love that existed within my family, and that it was not their fault. They could not be responsible for not giving something that they were not experiencing within themselves. To arrive within the lives of my parents so innocent and so pure, and then at times through my varied interpretations I began to experience life as harsh and cold. For many years I was overwhelmingly confused by the actions of certain members of my family who were in dential of the roles they played in sabotaging my self-esteem and completely tormenting my mind with harsh comments, a lack of guidance and the blatant refusal to be responsible for loving me. At times I felt I was someone who just lived in their home.

I appreciate that we all have a different capacity to both express love and live love. However, I see today that we need to be responsible for increasing our capacity to give and receive love. Especially when we are honored to have children. Especially if you have come from a life that has not necessarily provided love that honors your childhood. Love is what we must strive to find—first within ourselves.

$\mathcal{W}$ho Am I?

What a brave question: "Who am I?" I mean, do we really want to know? I know I didn't. I was a time bomb of negative thought processes about myself, waiting to go off. I was looking for an excuse to explode—the victim volcano, overflowing with the lava of anger and depression and finding many ways to deny who I truly was based on fear of knowing my True-self.

The Big Question

For many years throughout my life I was completely confused about the concept of knowing myself. The imbalance of not knowing myself projected inconsistency into my life; I was a seesaw of negative programming. When I was first prompted from deep within to ask myself the empowering question, "Who am I?" I was immediately taken on a wonderful ride of self-discovery, guided all the way by the ancient wisdom within my heart. This voice picked up the woman, the girl, the daughter and nurtured her into the pleasure of being a woman. By accepting this guidance and taking action I began to experience incredible courage. Suddenly accepting myself and seeking my True-self became exciting, and the challenge became a constant flow of victory. What I had feared so much quickly became the most uplifting experience ever. In accepting who I was my mind became disinterested in self-criticism. Learning to identify with fear and Truth and fearlessly following the path and understanding of Truth is so simple because it is so nurturing.

The most empowering decision I have ever made in my life has been to follow the voice of my heart—the nurturing voice of unconditional love, the voice that encourages you through life as the most divine, loving mother. The decision to follow this voice took me into the depths of deep love for myself, where I met my inner child and nursed her like a mother of true companionship. Where I accepted responsibility to give love to others. Where I accepted my responsibility to provide a home of love, balance, joy and friendship for my children. Where as a woman I am able to provide unconditional love and attract softness and awareness from within a man. Based on the level of my transformation I now see this question as the gate to the heart. Being consciously aware of your self-transformation will turn the key to this gate. Upon opening this gate a flooding river of inner wisdom will nurture you as your most nurturing companion of truth. The one question I was most afraid to answer was the one question that funneled new life within my heart, abundantly teaching my mind and nurturing every aspect of myself.

Today I love knowing who I am, because I am continuously re-creating who I am into a woman of higher knowing and golden values. With conscious breathing I have taken every aspect of who I found myself to be and re-created life into an experience of higher learning, transforming the misinterpretations of pain into the joy of acceptance. So who am I? Ask yourself: "Am I happy? Happy to be me? To learn what I have had to? Am I happy to face what I have to overcome?" Be relieved that you have the inner strength and determination to overcome the hurdles of the negative thought processes dictating your life. You will be overcome with joy knowing that you can turn your life around and re-create it to be an expression of joy based on your faith and understanding of your inner world.

The sooner you believe this, the more quickly you will be empowered to overcome all of the obstacles in your life.

Humorous Self

If there is one thing that you will discover on the path to self-awareness, it is that a sense of humor is vital when you are consciously re-creating your subconscious thinking and your life. Taking everything too seriously will and can create a short-lived discipline. To completely integrate self-love, you will at times need to accept self-transformation in the wisdom of humor. When you do this, in time you will experience the most unique sense of humor residing within your heart. When you are sifting through who you are, have that little giggle. As much as it is vital to understand who we are, accepting who we are comes around much more quickly through humor. Through joining in union with the humor within your heart you will not only experience love for who you are, but you will appreciate getting to know who you are.

When discovering the lessons behind your experiences, the first step is to be aware of the experiences that create the most disharmony for you. Then in that awareness, together with your inner guidance, accept the experience and allow your heart to nurture the aspect of yourself that is realizing the interpretation. You can successfully accomplish this by not allowing your inner grief to overshadow your inner joy. Learn that there is beauty in taking the tragedy and owning it, expressing it as a highest teaching and an aspect of pure love. Today when I reflect back through my life, when I see what has changed and how I have changed, I know that I am accomplishing self-transformation.

From my accomplishment I experience inner joy; I experience exactly who I am in my most empowered understanding. This is an experience available to us all. The experience of holding one's power and merging within the inner joy of a heart radiating truth. How do we achieve this connection? We inhale into it. We expand our new understanding into our lives through breath. We inhale, we know. We inhale, we experience. We inhale, we are peace, acceptance, knowing and celebration.

Accepting Who We Are

The most difficult time in my life was from age sixteen to twenty-six. This was a time of my life in which I was mental and emotional chaos. It was almost as if I had short-circuited mentally, emotionally and physically. I had no reasoning or understanding of life in general. My gravest fear was facing my grief and the challenge of overcoming chronic depression. It was during this time that I began to abuse myself with drugs, food, alcohol and sex. I was completely lost and devastatingly sad. I felt worthless, and everything in my life — including my relationships, prosperity and physical condition — said that I was worthless, further empowering my desperate state of chronic depression. I was living the life of an inner child shattered with betrayal and becoming a woman consumed in this betrayal. Accepting who I was seemed out of my reach. I had no concept of how I was going to heal myself when I found out who I was. My mind fearing change, telling me I could not get around what would happen when I said, "I was a nut case on a path of destruction."

When I began practices that awakened my understanding and sent forth the ancient wisdom from within my heart, my mind was overwhelmed by the disciplined education it received from my heart. My heart abundantly provided the constant assistance and methods to overcome issues. All I had to do was accept that mentally I could not heal my life. I needed help. I had to believe in the inner experience that was presenting itself to me. I had to believe in the inner strength and courage that was shining in the brilliant light of self-transformation.

I further invoked this belief in myself through my action of conscious breathing, which re-created my life to be an expression of Truth and a healing sanctuary of light. Reading through the following journal entry, I today see how acutely depressed my mind had been and how absolutely necessary it had been that my life change. Depression would have ended my life through suicide.

The action of suicide is not something we can control in the minute of doing such a thing. That is why it is vital that life is a life of higher understanding and not of confusion, to embrace your life and your experiences. My father had committed suicide after destroying his life with drugs. He was denying his pain and the violence that he demonstrated daily to both himself and others. So in my mind the victim had the perfect reason and excuses for suicide, until I saw that the victim only wanted help and that help was to identify with inner beauty. Through my seven attempts of suicide my victim had been crying out for help to heal the excruciating pain that we experience when we live without self-worth.

Who Am I?

Journal Entry, April 1996

As I sit staring out into the ocean, I ask the question, Why? Where is this life taking me? The pain inside, the shattered child, ripped-off adolescent and acutely depressed adult. Where is the happiness? Why have I experienced such physical punishment and why do I now live with the coldness of a heart that is locked shut and feels as dark as a dungeon that has never been opened? I feel disassociated from everyone and everything in my life. I look at the ocean wanting to jump into the rippling waters and disappear within the color of the deepest depths.

To disappear and never awaken, that is the desire I have at times, especially now. As I wear my depression and feelings of abandonment as a physical cloak and mask.

Slowly tears begin to stream down my face. For I am a tear. I am the tears of yesterday, today and tomorrow. To cry a tear into the waters of the ocean and continue until all life has drained from my body, that would be my relief.

I feel completely lost. What is the meaning of life? Is it for suffering physical, mental and sexual abuse? Today I am twenty-six years old and I see no future. All I feel within is terror, shame and abandonment. I cry loudly, screaming out in pain. Nobody deserves such pain. The anger slowly surfacing for the amount of times I have attempted to take my life and not succeeded. What seems like further punishment? The temptation to leave and not the strength to carry through. If there were a God why would he wish me to stay and deal with further torment?

Will I ever escape the torment? My memories torment me, my inner enemies torment me, my abusers continue to torment me. All of the abuse eating away my heart.

I do not feel as though I am a whole person. I have too many shattered relationships within me. I am begging for help, freedom and peace. In seeking this resolution I have made regular visits to my psychiatrist for the past four years. A kind, gentle, sensitive man has sat with me twice a week and attempted to cheer me up. How could anybody cheer me up? How can they extract all of the bad memories, programming and habits of abuse from within me? If so, then I would be cured and life would be happy. Through the life that I have lived I no longer believe in miracles.

"Time for a joint." An inhale of escape. The peace pipe, as it was known in ancient times. A peace pipe to me. As it is a tool to escape the pain. The deeper the pain the bigger the joint. At times I have been completely void for days in the bliss of smoke. But from this high my body feels unfit and out of balance. As the more I puff the less I care. I do not care to change issues and let go of my grief. For as long as I continue to inhale this addiction there is less chance that I will completely deal with what exists within and truly honor who I am as a person. Honor! Where could I have learned that word? It is certainly not from my life's experience.

I remember this time during which I cried out to the universe for help. I had done it many times throughout my life in a screaming desperation, but this time I was humble. I was on my knees. "I am ready," I said. "Is anyone there?" The pain had to be over. I was filled to the top with grief.

I was desperate to finally be free of this grief—to understand who I was, not who I had become. To locate some inner gentleness, somewhere within. In many ways sexual abuse makes you feel hard, disconnected from the gentleness of your female self. It is very obvious to you that in the presence of other women you do not feel like a whole woman, and you can easily identify with your masculine imbalance. I needed to be free from this feeling. I needed to finally understand how I could function in a healthy, balanced way physically, mentally and emotionally. Every day I became more and more desperate to find some peace, begging to leave behind the trauma that I seemed to relive daily.

The day I asked and invoked this healing I had no idea what I was asking. I had no concept of the act of spiritually calling yourself back. I had never heard of it. But I knew from the pit of my stomach that this is what I had to do. I knew that part of me was missing from my life. However, I was completely unaware mentally of how to achieve this. This simplicity and, at the time, ignorance I today see as one of my greatest gifts. This ignorance allowed me to be guided by my heart. I could not answer the questions to transform myself and accomplish the action mentally; I had to completely surrender to the action of the heart to succeed. It demonstrated to me the only aspect of myself that understood what was happening and what I had to do to completely turn my life around and nurse my wounds.

Throughout the process of this transformation within my mind I knew to keep it simple, to listen to the guidance within my heart and follow it. After some time my mind witnessed this process of transformation, and it would at times challenge the heart. But no matter how difficult it was for my mind to believe that the heart action was the action I was to take, I took it. I looked for resistance, watching my mind make its little suggestions to try and remove me from my empowered state. I could easily determine when this was happening, because the action that it was suggesting would align me to an old way of thinking. It would align me to a repeat experience or outcome, and I would be saying, "Why do I feel this way?" It would make suggestions of why I should not forgive or have compassion for another or why I was not beautiful and deserving of unconditional love.

My mind did not always put forward a challenge. It only did so in times it felt that it would be tiring to change, that it would miss out on something or when it was afraid and felt vulnerable. At these times, that which my mind usually felt was the right action was the opposite of what my heart encouraged me to do.

I had lived with bouts of depression. I knew the difference between negative criticism and positive change. The voice within my heart encouraged me to slow down, to be conscious of my thoughts. It encouraged me to contemplate my actions, making suggestions of peace and love. Forgiveness rang through in all of my steps in healing my past actions. An important step to empowering the heart is not to overload on too much information about changing. Just simply want it, and surrender to the divine light within. Use what you learn outside of yourself as a tool to finding what is within. Have no expectation of your spiritual self. I saw that in doing this, my mind was not given the opportunity, through too much knowledge, to mimic steps of the heart. I had a system. If I needed strength, courage or wisdom to accomplish a change in myself, I would ask my heart. I would sit down in a spare moment, and I would ask. I would agree in my request to honor my transformation, and I would accept to move forward. I developed incredible trust for believing in myself and my capacity to bring within myself all that I needed to fully merge within my heart.

An example of this was the spontaneous healing experience that took place in April of 1996, when I was taking a nice warm bath one evening. I placed my hands on my stomach and I began to breathe. I said, "No more. Please, help. No longer can pain and memories continue to sabotage my life."

I felt choked in the throat, suppressing all my grief. I began to stroke my legs downward, pushing away as if brushing something off my body. I remained in that bath for a long time, simply inhaling the golden light from the candles. It was in this moment that I met my determination. I touched briefly on my will to transform my life. I trusted in calling out in this way, and this was vital. Do you know why I trusted? I had to. I knew through my life's experiences that nothing I had done so far had helped me a great deal. I let go to the point at which I was calling out in desperation, because I had nowhere else to go other than within.

As I sat quietly after my bath I contemplated life without the baggage. I ached to smile and for anyone, including me, to know that I was worth respect and nurturing, that I was worth saving. Deep within myself I mourned the loss of my childhood and the comfort that a family provides when you face the challenges of being a young woman. I had been on my own for nine years at this point, and I still experienced acute anxiety from the separation from my parents and the issues that brought the separation about. I crawled through life in humiliation from my interpretation that I was not worthy to be with them. Desperately I ached to live without the constant interpretation of this pain as well as many others—without the memories and the destructive thoughts for myself. In that sacred bath I breathed deeply, consciously paying attention to each breath and the intention of inhaling my wish for self-transformation.

This was the first night of an incredible story, a story I will continue to share with you as a key of inspiration on your path of self-transformation.

For many hours after my bath I sat in silence, consciously breathing and creating a synchronicity of mind, breath and vision of my life transformed. Captivated in this vision, I lay down on my bed, continuing to inhale and exhale and invoking conscious transformation. When I awoke in the morning I had experienced the most incredible dream of my life, a dream that numbed me with anticipation for three years.

A Dream of Love

I had seen myself lying restful on my bed in the early hours of the morning. The most brilliant ray of light had poured through the roof and was shining directly on me while I slept. Slowly I began to rise up, out of my bed, out of the building, climbing higher and higher into the stars.

Being drawn upward I remained within the ray of light, continuing to float higher and higher. As I looked across the sky there was another ray of light, just like the one in which I was floating. A ray of light carrying another person—a man. I watched him climb higher and higher at exactly the same speed as I did.

Eventually we arrived at the base of the sun, and slowly we began to circle the sun, side by side, around and around the base of the sun. We moved closer and closer together, until we were facing one another. We continued to revolve around the sun in a magnificent golden ray of light.

Slowly we moved together, and our foreheads pressed together. We continued to circle the sun pressed up against one another, in perfect harmony and synchronicity, his presence captivating and silent.

In the next moment we began to spin. Spinning and spinning within a golden ray of light we proceeded toward the ground. In the stream of light, continuing to spin, we moved closer and closer to a perfectly round rock pool sitting on the most magnificent golden sand. As we got quite close to the ground our bodies transformed into a sparkling stream of water. This beautiful sparkling stream abundantly poured forth from within the golden light. As the water poured from the light toward the ground it filled the magnificent rock pool. As the sacred water filled this rock pool not a ripple formed. Not a bubble or a stir. The water was completely still.

In the next moment of the dream I was flying through the sky as a young child of six, holding hands with a small boy the same age. We were flying through the night sky over cities and countries, laughing and giggling. I was encouraging this little boy to open up to life. To experience the freedom of the heart—the freedom of joy, to come with me on a journey of self-discovery. I explained to him in childish fun that we had agreed to make this transformation. He cried out, "It's too hard, too difficult, I don't want to do it." "Oh yes, you do," I had said. "It's time to meet all of you, and this is what we are both going to do. The strength is within and the time is now.

This was our agreement and *you* think that it's been hard. Come on, we're doing this." My inner child was giggling at this most sweet little boy and his doubts of transformation, exasperated by my acceptance to change. It ended.

When I awoke from this dream I was different. The whole night had made me different—my calling out for self-transformation in the bath and then this magnificent dream. The rock pool was in my heart. For months later I could sit for hours connecting to the soul that had traveled to the sun with me. It was the most magnificent and empowering dream I have ever had. This dream answered the question, and truthfully I was shown who I was. I had asked who I was, asked for help to find the peace. I wanted an experience without the pain, and I got it. That rock pool and its tranquility nurtured me throughout the next three years, and one day I connected with that sacred soul who had circled the sun with me. In our coming together I connected with the tranquility and the oneness of the water. I found the little boy I encouraged in the dream on the day when, as a woman, I merged into love. The Complete Earthly Woman merged with the Complete Earthly Man. This was an abundant gift in my life that I will share with you later. I have to save the best until last.

*H*eal the Sexuality of the Abused Child and the Self-Abused Woman

Throughout my life I have been actively involved in experiences of sexual intimacy while denying the beauty of my own sexuality. Due to my childhood experiences, I was making painful sexual choices by the time I became a young woman. I was making the choices that empowered my sexual grief, and this perpetuated my worthlessness. I was desperate to attract love through the experience of sexual intimacy, yet it proved never to be the case. Sex became a way to punish every aspect of myself. My inner child was uncomfortable and afraid of sexual intimacy. I always seemed to attract partners who stimulated this fear, even if the fear was the repeat occurrence that the man would walk from my life, after experiences of intimacy. I became bedroom material and not girlfriend material.

To my adolescent self, the men I attracted empowered her acute loneliness and confirmation that she was worthless. Men would sense my depressed state of mind and run a mile. By the time I had become a young woman I was filled and overflowing with self-hatred and confusion in seeking the perfect male. When I began addressing my sexual issues I began to tap into a well of grief that awaited realization. I was breathless with pain. I had taken so harshly rejection by others. I had interpreted the ego of the male to be hard and self-centered. I thought that men only sought one thing and they sought it with me because I had expected that they would. So when I finally began to address my sexual interpretations, the most amazing realization I made, was that my whole life, and the people in it, were an exact reflection of my sexual grief. When I realized this and consciously sought to address and remove my negative interpretations, my life dramatically changed in every single aspect.

Our Choice in Partners

It is so important that you choose your sexual partners with caution. Only seek a sacred experience with one who will reflect your best qualities. Know that when you share sexual energy with another you can actually take on that person's energy, storing it within the sexual organs and your body's sexual fibers. These sexual fibers are stored within your cellular memory as energy, so after the sexual act expect to see your partner in your actions and hear them in your thoughts. Often it is hard to know when this energy exchange has happened within yourself, because these thoughts will reflect themselves as thoughts you have of yourself. I have spoken to many people who have had the physical experience of storing some of their partner's energy in their physical bodies.

One woman told me a story about her relationship with a gentlemen suffering from bouts of depression. After some time in the relationship, she began to feel physically exhausted. This exhaustion became so serious that she developed an acute pain in her shoulders and was at the point of having to resign from her job. She visited a specialist who, as he was trying to uncover her problem, asked about her boyfriend. After a lengthy discussion he advised her that her boyfriend's depression was the source of her problem. Her energy was being affected by his lack of life force energy. She explained to me that she had spent a great deal of time trying to help her boyfriend overcome his issues; however, he was disinterested, and eventually she left him. Within days she began to return to normal.

After practicing consciously re-creating her sexual interpretations of this relationship and releasing her expectations of the relationship through conscious breathing, she is well on her way to being fully restored energetically and abundantly nurtured by her heart. Leaving him was not necessarily the answer. Simply being aware of her absorbing his depression and changing her intention toward him may have been enough. If he was consciously trying to re-create his life and her as well, his depression may have been transformed; however, she would have been able to remove it through conscious breathing and her intention that he heal. Since he was denying his role in the situation it made it difficult to heal what was taking place and left her no option but to leave.

So you see that it is vital when we share ourselves sexually with another that we consciously and truthfully own our experience with that person. How many times have you been in a situation (or known of one) in which you do not truthfully accept your partner's negative behavior by continuously making excuses for it? Suddenly the person making excuses for the behavior becomes more weakened, emotionally and mentally, by the person who is serving up the behavior. This is because when we are faced with truth and we deny it we fall into the suffering of denial. Then comes resentment that we put up with the behavior. In this situation love of self is the only action that will allow the truth to come out. If you truly love yourself then accepting behavior that is not good for your existence becomes unacceptable. By striving to love yourself, negative relationships and accepting negative treatment will fall away as ash. From my personal experience in working with myself and other women, conscious breathing is incredibly precise and effective in clearing cellular memory and that which can be stored during intimate relationships. Conscious breathing allows you to re-create your sexual energy—every minute of every day.

What is Your Experience?

Within this chapter we will re-create and redefine the term sexual abuse and refer to this type of experience as "an experience of sexual discomfort." We will do this for the purpose of bringing together as many different women and issues as possible.

Take a moment to reflect quietly within to make your inner connection to your experience of sexual discomfort. Seek within yourself and understand that it is not so much the circumstances of your experiences but your interpretation of them that impact you. Move within and see if you have reacted negatively to a sexual experience and created negative sexual behavior or patterning within your personality. Does your inner child or does your life reflect any experience of sexual discomfort? Do you ever have moments of anxiety with who you are and your beauty and ability as a woman? Or are you simply experiencing different stages of discomfort in your role as a woman? We will re-create these issues in this moment, removing the unappreciated sexual experience simply by accepting that it is time to draw boundaries with how you conduct yourself sexually. Taking this step is the first step in healing your sexuality and is important to transforming your life and empowering your intuition. Make the conscious decision to accept your past sexual experiences with understanding and love. Cease criticizing yourself and cease to continue creating the same patterns through misguided choices. Whatever your sexual experiences, this chapter will either help you or somebody that you know.

In all of the many woman I have met, I honestly have yet to meet a woman who has not experienced some form of sexual discomfort, either as a result of her own choices or as the repercussions of another person's actions. Changing your interpretations of sex and empowering your sexuality is easy, because it is the "in" thing. There are many resources and a great deal of support available. Consider yourself not alone in a world of transformation—only alone in the world of denial.

Determining Issues—Creating Boundaries

There are many types of experiences of sexual discomfort, and when we speak of setting up boundaries it is difficult to see this as a helpful step in the experience of rape or sexual molestation. These are two experiences in which your boundaries seem useless. In these circumstances it would seem no help at all to have boundaries. If you have experienced any type of sexual violation, drawing healthy boundaries after the experience can be very difficult. Stemming from the fact that your boundaries were violated; as a repercussion of this violation confusion can establish itself as part of your process in identifying or creating healthy boundaries. So how do we establish and create healthy sexual boundaries after any experience of sexual discomfort or to protect us from any future experience of sexual discomfort? Simple. Ask yourself these questions you can determine your boundaries.

1. Do I want to sexually share myself with this person for the first time under the influence of any substance—even alcohol?

2. In sharing a sexual experience with this person am I growing in a positive, healthy way sexually?

3. Through this experience will I learn to identify and appreciate my sexuality more than I do today?

4. Do I want to exchange physical energy with the other person?

5. Who wants to have a sexual experience? Do I or does the other person?

6. Through my behavior towards the other person have I provoked this situation, or is it something that we each wish to experience as much as the other?

Until you become comfortable establishing sexual boundaries during the initial stages of your transformation, I suggest that you use these examples of sexual boundaries so as not to re-create the same issues. Eventually, after getting to know yourself and the empowered self within, you will more than likely reestablish your boundaries. Through making the transformation to evaluate relationships and sexual activity through healthy boundaries, you are well on the way to empowering your sexuality for the pleasure of yourself. After implementing your boundaries your sexuality will become an inner silence where your heart can begin to speak to your mind, healing it of all past experiences of sexual discomfort and guiding it into future sexual experiences of sacred oneness.

When you begin to work on healing yourself and bringing forward your sacred female beauty, your boundaries will both protect and nurture your new sense of wholeness. Begin by seeing your new level of understanding as a seedling budding within your heart. Your boundaries are the fence. They act as the protection for your precious bud so that it will blossom into a magnificent flower of understanding and self-empowerment. You will see that boundaries will make you feel special, confident and abundantly in love with yourself.

By setting boundaries, you begin to reestablish your values. Values are a vital contributing factor to turning your life around. Values say, "I value me. I value what I offer another. I value that I am a sacred woman." A mantra to further empower your values and help build strength in acting on your values is: *My values take me into my deepest, most sacred aspect of truth.* In time, after experiencing your life turning around, this mantra will replace your negative thoughts and choices. Values never empower a negative thought, only a positive step toward empowering our self-esteem and positions within our lives.

Re-create Your Sexuality Through Conscious Breathing

Whatever your sexual experience, you will see through your own acceptance and the conscious breathing purification process that you can transform yourself sexually. By disciplining your thoughts, you can successfully align all sexual experiences to the act of spiritual learning in which the guilt and fear will dissolve.

You will triumph over the process of owning your experiences. Now is the time to realize that sexual experiences can effectively point out to us many different aspects of our personalities and behavior. Seek the understanding within your inner guidance that every sexual experience you have ever had has played an important role in your life, because sexual experiences allow you to identify with how you want to be as a person, what you value and what is right for you. Doing this also determines how you feel about sexual intimacy and your participation as well as your capacity to give satisfying, unconditional love to another.

When you go within, silently ask yourself how you feel about yourself sexually. While reflecting on past experiences, make your conclusions as impersonal as possible. Do you blame another or yourself? Do you look for something that should have been that was not? Just look at your reaction to the experience as the experience was. When you see your reaction, are you re-creating this reaction through other experiences and relationships? Do you set up experiences and relationships in your life that have you react in the same way you did after an uncomfortable sexual experience? I will give you an example. In my childhood I always felt out of place with other children, generally with other people. As a teenager, I was begging for mercy inside. Humiliation was eating me away as I lived with the memory and knowing of my childhood sexual experiences. Therefore, I was so afraid of myself and the intense grief within that I had to laugh the most, be the loudest, be the most alert and crack the most jokes. This behavior made me untouchable. I was petrified of people—of them discovering my fear for life. I did not want them to see my depression, because they might ask why I had it.

I had to behave in a way that made them stay as far away as possible from my secret. Throughout my life I invoked many close calls of rape and assault while consistently facing sexual dishonesty, self-betrayal and self-violation. My worst experiences were dictating my entire life.

Throughout all of my experiences and relationships, each one was saying, "Face who you are, know yourself and begin to love yourself." I was taken through so many negative experiences while denying my pain that in the end I was begging for mercy. I was aching for love, firstly from myself. Then came the further discomfort that as much as I was hiding who I was, I was constantly being challenged, because the manner in which I conducted myself socially, deceptively showed me to be a strong woman, a person who could deal with the knocks. This was far from the truth. I finally resented my life so intensely that I began to react to my life and those around me in the same aggressive, angry way in which I reacted to myself in my early childhood. I was never outwardly angry or upset with my circumstances, just petrified and crawling with self-hatred. So by the time I was an adult, I felt others in my life were violating my relationship with them, because they did not really know who I was. I had not allowed them to, and I therefore resented what I had created.

The point that I am coming to is that by identifying with issues that are based on your sexual discomfort, you will begin to see these issues in many areas of your life such as relationships, prosperity, self-worth, sexuality, self-criticism, self-acceptance and your ability to move forward into new experiences. This is completely normal.

However, there comes a time to re-create the programming

and to remove intense pain. A time to move into understanding. I knew that my negative subconscious programming came from sexual abuse. Some women have, through other negative experiences, relived the repercussions of those experiences through their sexual choices. The reflection of their negative subconscious programming is from unrelated sexual experiences and is lived out through their negative sexual choices. Either way, healing any sexual dysfunction is vital. If this is what you would like to do, then it is simple. Through the action of conscious breathing you can exhale all of your sexual experiences that you see as imbalanced and inhale your sexual values, the sexual invocations of the Complete Earthly Woman. If you want to successfully clear your negative programming, you will need to take some time out to practice inhaling and exhaling the invocations. In this way you will re-create your sexual energy. You will touch on peace within and be self-empowered in the process.

As you progress into the invocations, read through them and inhale each line as you read. When you exhale, close your eyes. Then reopen your eyes and inhale the next line, and so on. From this simple connection through conscious breathing you will feel connected to your most empowered self and will further invoke the presence of the Complete Earthly Woman.

If you want to successfully clear your negative programming, you will need to take some time out to practice inhaling and exhaling the invocations to re-create your sexual energy.

However, for this moment I suggest to you that you read over each invocation in Transforming Sexuality (page 40). Read through each of the seven invocations provided, practicing to inhale each line of each invocation whilst exhaling all resistance. (For further explanation refer to Chapter 2.) From this simple practice you will invoke peace and self-empowerment within.

Give yourself this experience as a most incredible gift. Self-transformation and cleansing the cellular memory and the mind are this simple. I encourage you to both believe it and do it. You will find an abundant resource of self-worth within by simply believing in yourself—believing that you can transform your thinking mind and empower your heart through such beauty as the invocations and through such simplicity as breathing. You will see that the further along the path of inner transformation you travel, the fuller your heart and the richer your life will become.

Honoring Your Inner Child

For many of us, the expression of sexuality can be a tight knot of confusion. This is because existing within is an inner child with specific views on sexuality based on experience. Changing the perception of the child that has lived experiences of sexual discomfort is an important step and can be successful when using breathing and imagery, because they are two aspects of your self-empowerment journey in which the child can participate and understand.

The age at which experiences of sexual discomfort have taken place in your life is irrelevant. The inner child has been either a participant or a witness, and either way she is carrying the scars and confusion of the experience. It is critical to identify with the interpretations of this precious child, as there is no way that she will not have been affected by the trauma of the experience. The time is always right to take her by the hand and heal her, simply by teaching her that life can be different and that the way she sees life can be positive, joyous, nurturing and fun.

Our three-year-old daughter has been a master in teaching me how to heal my inner child. Through my experience with her I have identified with a key aspect in healing the little girl within. Communicating with our daughter has shown me to always encourage my inner child to take positive steps through explanation. If I encourage her through simplicity and excitement she is happy to follow my guidance, whereas if I simply implement change without explanation and without her input she will more than likely resist. The inner child must participate in the growth along the path of self-empowerment. In the instance of an interpretation such as trauma, the child must heal. To do this you must incorporate practices to which the child can relate based on her level of understanding and her capacity to participate.

Often when I have been counseling women, discussing the reunion with the inner child, they will say, "Sounds positive, but how do I connect with my inner child when I have my own children and I am always in the role of responsibility?"

Or people simply have difficulty at times integrating how they will reintroduce the essence of the inner child back into their lives as an adult. In answer to this question a wonderful and yet obvious technique presented itself to me: *Honoring the Inner Child*. Within us is a divine little person who can be seen as our boarding pass on this sacred journey of life. When did we forget to honor the innocence, the humility and the direct experience with incarnation that is part of this little person within us? It is so important as an adult that you take this little person by the hand into your heart. Nurture her by creating a life filled with safety through your practice of self-love and by establishing boundaries that honor her life within you.

To rebuild this connection with your inner child I suggest that you pick a peaceful, private place within your home and make a sacred space of honor for your inner child. In this sacred space you can place some pictures of you as a child—pictures that make you feel a twinge within when you look into the eyes of this precious little person. You may also like to place special little things that your inner child liked, such as books, songs, pictures—anything that was important to this special person. Now within this sacred space you are going to invoke your most sacred and empowering connection to this little person. For me the most simple, effective and empowering way to do this is through conscious breathing and invocation. I suggest lighting a beautiful candle to open the sacred space of your inner child. Then repeat the following sacred invocation out loud, telling your inner child that as an adult you provide this sacred space of expression where she can continue to express herself in the safety of your presence.

Begin by breathing in through your nose and out through your mouth, relaxing with each breath. Continue this practice in silence as you calm and silence your thoughts by focusing on your breathing. By doing this you will empower your invocation, focused on the feeling and inner connection to your inner child. Then repeat out loud:

On this sacred day in this sacred moment, I inhale inner unity and the whole connection within the essence of my inner child. As I am this inner child and I am the existence and essence of this inner child. As I continue to breathe deeply I inhale the beauty and conscious creation of this beloved child. As I continue to inhale I empower the union with this precious aspect of divinity. Within the essence of this sacred moment I look within and hold forward a nurturing hand that on this sacred day we may join as one. As within this sacred life I join in unity in the creation of the child and re-creation of the woman into the pure joyousness and simplicity of this precious child. As we live in union as one, beyond this day into tomorrow may we travel as a sacred union. As within this moment I hold you, divine one, within my arms—the arms of a nurturing woman—and I invoke you, precious child, to let go into this moment. All that suppresses you into the play of fear and self-doubt. Within this moment I ask you, precious little girl, to let go and to hand over within each breath so that you may live this life within the heart and within a life of abundant joy. As we come together and we are one, precious child.

I thank you for your courage. Here we will remain within the heart. I say to you now, precious girl, all that you are is innocence. Anything else is gone within each exhale. With this beautiful candle and in this beautiful place we make our place together where in safety we speak and come closer and closer and closer, into the essence of true self-love. I love you, precious, and welcome you within the arms of the Complete Earthly Woman. That which I become, that which I am.

At this point inhale a hug. Sit silently within this moment and contemplate this sacred union together. Inhale the warmth and sacredness of this moment.

You want your inner child to step out of the place where she has been waiting for you to reconnect with her. You want her to give to you all that she wishes to let go of and to experience that joyous freedom that is the essence of the pure child. Throughout the conscious practice of the breathing techniques, you will always be invoking the participation and union with the inner child. This moment of invocation with this precious child has been the awakening ceremony of your inner child—the first time you sit in this sacred space and invoke her presence. Awakening the connection to your inner child is another aspect of owning your actions and who you are. Owning the transformation that you want to make within your life. I encourage you, when you initially make this connection, to actively discipline yourself to sit in your sacred space with your inner child often, perhaps even daily.

Eventually you will move from practicing this exercise regularly, and you will grow into another aspect of your process. You will not have to sit daily to connect with your inner child; she will be very present in your life and all of your decisions and actions. Discipline and routine practice will be the most effective way to empower this union and dissolve any negative interpretations. Eventually it will not matter what situation you are in as an adult—you will both see and hear the inner child expressing her participation in your life. You will not look for her; you will be consciously connected, and at different times you will witness the joy, purity and reunion within your daily life as an adult. I encourage you to practice the *Honoring the Inner Child* conscious breathing technique (Chapter 2) each time you sit in your sacred space to honor your beloved inner child.

When the child has actively participated in releasing interpretations and experiences, when she has integrated into your adult mind her self-realizations, you will reach the point at which you will transform into your most empowered, developed, wisest being. You will be re-created as you eventually heal the repercussions of experiences of sexual discomfort as well as other issues that present themselves. You will turn any confusion, grief or guilt into your greatest teacher, through conscious breathing and imagery. You will thank all who have had an impact in your life for their participation in your experience of becoming a Complete Earthly Woman.

The Healing Line—Blood Line

Throughout the final steps of turning my life around I became aware that those who have appeared to have violated me the most are my most empowering spiritual teachers. It is through my association with these souls that I have gone deep within myself.

I have nurtured my inner child in the way that she has never been nurtured, and as a woman and a mother I have become a counselor and a best friend to my inner adolescent. I have integrated all of my different aspects as one, in union, balanced through conscious understanding. I was guided at the beginning of my transformation to look at different aspects of myself such as my inner adolescent and inner child. This assisted me to identify with their different issues, interpretations and confusion. During this process I saw how they had reflected one another. The adolescent, through my inner child union, has been able to identify with the fears and interpretations of the inner child that initiated her actions toward herself when experiencing sexuality. This shifts the guilt and replaces it with self-forgiveness and understanding within the adolescent. It heals the actions I took as an adolescent, which seemed at the time to be an extended action of abuse—self-abuse. This happened sexually as well as through the use of drugs and alcohol and within relationships with others.

After identifying with the release of the guilt, the path of self-forgiveness began to flow within my life from my heart. This allowed me to forgive all who participated. I became free.

I gave them a thank you and I received an abundance of wisdom and love from within my heart. Today this wisdom has set me free to such an empowered level of understanding that it is this wisdom that honors my life and my experiences. It always had, but I hear it now because I know that this sacred wisdom is now my truth. My inner child, my adolescent and the experience of my life today are one—fully integrated in union. By allowing my mind to reveal myself at different ages such as the inner child, inner adolescent and adult, I have allowed myself to be reunited within as one. After the inner child and the adolescent begin supporting one another, instead of resenting and working against one another, full integration occurs, and you experience an overwhelming self-appreciation for who you are. An expression of wisdom fills your heart with an abundance of understanding and forgiveness. You become pure self-empowerment.

This self-empowerment is present throughout your entire life. You ignite the flame of prosperity and abundance in all aspects of your life. You cease being afraid.

Sexuality of the Complete Earthly Woman

The radiant female sexuality of the Complete Earthly Woman. Who is she? Well, certainly she is not a prudish woman but a woman surrounded in boundaries of truth, love, integrity, trust, understanding and honor. She consciously participates in the growth of her own sexuality as a woman. She experiences sexuality that beats the drumbeat of Mother Earth.

She nurtures all involved in her sexuality with unconditional love, appreciation and honor. She accepts that she is an expression of her truth, and the clearer the truth the more it will manifest and create all experiences ignited in the beauty of sexuality to be the exchange of self-love.

It is a gift when you desire to go within. In this desire you are seeking to please yourself, to nurture yourself, to find who sits within and to find the woman who has not been betrayed. Find the woman who is not the victim, and find the woman who shines as a diamond as she walks upon Mother Earth. In finding this woman you allow her to prepare our children to heal society and nurture the masculine and feminine aspects of our Creation. This is when our female aspect is ascending the world into the heart of harmony. Any woman living in a world that is filled with misguided sexuality owes it to herself to find and become true, earthly, honored sexuality.

Sexuality to a woman who has had experiences of sexual discomfort becomes an experience of whole inner joy. When your inner female meets your inner male and in natural harmony forms oneness within the balance of Mother Earth. Alive within your heart as a Complete Earthly Woman. Nurtured within your stomach, your womb and sex. It is to look through a window into the song of nature and smile to yourself. It is to lay naked upon Mother Earth and feel yourself moving in and out of the sun. It is to let go of the baggage and glow with the face of an innocent child. It is to feel a comforting hand of unconditional love upon your shoulder. It is to move in a sacred dance, swirling, swaying and vibrating to the rhythm of Mother Earth.

It is to rock within the essence of Mother Earth, entwined in union with another precious soul who is also experiencing soul, heart, oneness. How do you find this life? You look within and you go for it. You cease to cry out as the victim that you do not have it. You rewrite the story with love, from *tragedy* to *triumph*.

I share with you in this moment this poem of appreciation for the time we have spent together in this chapter. Healing what has been spoken of in this chapter has taken me the most courage and transformed my life in the greatest way. I thank you for this sacred moment of sharing this with you. I give to you from my heart the vow that conscious breathing and the sexuality invocations provided will change your life through you believing in yourself. If this is difficult, then believe in what is here, as eventually this practice will take you to your self-belief through your confirmation of your own self-transformation.

One day I looked in the mirror and I held my breath,
choked by the humiliation of a life of violated sexuality,
a part of me inside cringing,
hiding in the darkness of impurity.
This is what I was—violated impurity.

One day I looked in the mirror and I breathed,
inhaled my inner beauty—
the true magnificence of being a woman.
A part of me awoke inside.
I stood up.
I looked at myself.
I cried.
One day I looked in the mirror
I inhaled deep within myself,
I am beautiful.
I am the purity of the most graceful swan.
I am as thankful as the most gracious soul.
As within my heart I am a
Complete Earthly Woman

Sacred Union

To be a woman is to be humble,
spiritually nurturing the soul,
the soul of Mother Earth
through spiritual practice,
actions, thoughts, words and
deeds of integrity.
As within each breath I take
I merge within the divinity
of the woman.
The heart.
That which I am.

Self-esteem
is the inner beauty
that enables you to give
wisdom and Truth to all

Chapter 7

Behold the essence Mother Earth
within your womb,
her beauty within your heart.
Consciously merge with her in oneness.
Close your eyes,
inhale the most beautiful picture of her
you can create.
"Peaceful is a woman of nature."

∾   ∾   ∾

Society's Women

Have women lost their place upon the sacred mantel? Some of us have forgotten that as men and women we are sacred temples. Either we have forgotten or have been removed from this inner knowledge through life's circumstances. However, this is exactly where we belong — upon the sacred mantel, worshipped as the beauty of the earth, the beauty of life. It is unrealistic to expect society to do this for us. It must be achieved within our own lives first. Then as a natural flow, how you see yourself is how others will see you. Just as women have been used for pleasure within the mind of our society, so has Mother Earth. She has been abused for convenience, greed, jealousy and technology. The repercussions of this lack of purity within the female energy of the planet has polluted the male aspect of this planet, and as a result there is much grief and disharmony.

At the appropriate time in our history women suppressed their femininity by living a more male role. Men also suppressed their feminine side as society had them do it. Society said, "You don't need to know yourself when you are a man.

You don't have time, and nobody is interested. Make money, and make a life for yourself." In this, all lost touch in the need to honor women. Honoring the sacred woman is a vital quality of the Complete Earthly Woman, the aspect of being a woman that has been suppressed.

From what I know today, when all women join in one group consciousness of self-transformation, the entire global consciousness of women and honor of the sacred woman will manifest into a direction of higher values for humanity. Women and their daughters will rise up and nurture the male aspect into the journey with simplicity and love. Why would we as women want to deny ourselves the true experience of complete honor in our roles as women? No matter where you come from, no matter what your material experiences or relationship experiences, move on. Move into the heart. Seek nothing but honor and respect. It is a lack of self-worth that wants to turn on a room full of egos seeking distasteful entertainment.

These discussions on the female role are not judgments— they are truth. It is not that your experiences before becoming the sacred qualities of truth are negative. They have served their purpose. They are what you had to experience along the path of self-discovery. However, we discuss them in terms of good and bad because nurturing and honoring the woman always makes us feel satisfied, happy and in the experience of self-love. Everything outside of this leaves us to question our motives and our experience.

The Sacred Woman

We cannot deny that society has forgotten that women are sacred. Most women themselves also forget this at some point in their lives. Hearing this, are you sensing your duty to honor this sacredness and love this sacredness? The duty of humanity is to see your sacredness and create an environment in which you can exist as this sacredness. If you really want to empower yourself, then really get to know yourself. Seek to both love and honor the sacred You.

Give away the false perceptions that create confusion in your role of being a woman by committing to yourself that you are an example of unconditional love to humanity. Show through your behavior, action and lifestyle that you are sacred ground. Why not? Isn't this what you have really wanted to hear? To finally connect to what you seek, the ancient heritage of being a woman. Are you aching to experience your life as an expression of unconditional love within your heart? This is an existence in which you are abundantly guiding others within their own hearts through example, trust and honorable companionship. In which all women, within their hearts, *want* all women to exist as beautiful reflections of the soul. In which society dissolves the issue of comparativeness of female beauty: in which women cease to challenge one another by turning beauty into a competition. Shouldn't we as women want all women to express their inner beauty, to come together in union? If a woman is denying her beauty, shouldn't we be offering a hand of pure love? How can a woman look at another female and criticize her physical, mental or emotional beauty? Every woman is beautiful, no matter what her circumstances. When you see a woman who appears to be struggling with her self-worth and her self-esteem, smile at her in your heart. In your heart and your purest intention send her a big bouquet of love. Pray silently within that the veils of ignorance that blind her of her own beauty fall away and that as a woman she merge within the magnificence of her self-love.

It may not be her physical appearance that projects her lack of self-love, but it may be the manner in which she relates to you or others, or it may be her emotional state. In whatever way she demonstrates a lack of whole to you, send her love from your heart as a true female companion. Remember, when you meet another woman, that sometimes in our lives we face challenges that are both uncomfortable for us and those around us; therefore, it is best not to judge those we meet. Because often what we judge today, we are tomorrow.

If you are afraid of seeing other people's pain and would be more comfortable either judging or criticizing them, then that action reflects your true feelings of yourself. You are afraid of yourself and who you are inside. You do not want to see your pain, and you would rather judge somebody else than accept that you must change yourself. When you begin to discipline your thoughts on criticizing and seeking faults in others, you will see that through giving compassion and pure intention to another you will empower your connection to your own heart. This empowerment carries through the process of accepting all that you are and all that you seek to change within your own life.

Men Say, "What Role Do I Play?"

Through the conversations I have had with many men in the last couple of years, I have identified with a confusion that exists within the minds of some men. This confusion eventuates from the changes that have taken place within society and the role of women. At times women will play the role of an independent female; at times demanding equality with men. Then in the next breath they look at men and say, "Nurture me and see my vulnerability. I am a little girl who needs kindness and for you to care for me with tenderness." The balance is missing.

The pendulum of women is swinging. If women lead the way through disciplined values and play their sacred female role from within their hearts, then the earthly males will elevate from their confusion and the behavior that is detrimental to the survival of the sacred female. This requires basing relationships on the qualities of unconditional love and compassion. The mass consciousness of men must rise to the understanding that women are sacred, and this can be initiated by women honoring themselves.

Men need to be nurtured by empowered women. When men see that women give sacred nurturing they will in return provide the nurturing for the sacred woman.

They will honor women in the way that is that of the true earthly man. In this experience women will take all men by the hand into their own hearts. This type of transformation is not for all men, as it is not for all women. It is not up to anybody to judge or criticize who makes a transformation within and who does not. It is not for some; they do not seek it. Their transformation may come about in a different way, as everyone's process is their own perfect road to self-realization.

Relationships

It is far too easy to have one negative experience with a person and expect all experiences and people to be the same. Begin using your relationships to empower your female side and nurture your male side while striving to merge within the magnificence of the Complete Earthly Woman.

Remember that a Complete Earthly Woman is your most empowered self. She does not belong in any specific type of relationship. She belongs in your life, where you exist as one. She will happily move in and out of many and all relationships that empower you to your divine Truth. It is vital when you do initiate your transformation that you draw boundaries immediately to protect what you seek. Create an environment that is safe for your transformation. This may mean changing some aspects of your life.

This may seem like a lot at times, but after the action is taken the self-empowerment is phenomenal. Courage is what will allow you to both invoke and carry through with change. This courage is given freely and abundantly when you demonstrate to the heart, to the Complete Earthly Woman, that you are seriously initiating your transformation through commitment and discipline in what you re-create in your life. It is both frustrating and confusing to face issues while making a transition and then swing like a pendulum, going back into old patterns. Discipline is the vital ingredient for progressing through inner transformation. It is discipline that will empower your awareness to identify and transform past and present issues.

Self-discipline and self-love will abundantly transform your self-esteem. In turn you will provide an abundance of love for others by making this commitment to yourself. The first relationship to master is your inner relationship with your True self. Learn to honor, respect and provide unconditional love through your actions for your True self in this relationship, and you will provide this abundance of love and wisdom in all of your relationships with both men and women.

ରୟ ରୟ ରୟ

An *Inner* Healing Retreat

At some point after we begin transforming our lives, we ache for that sacred time removed from the pressures and commitments of our normal routine. However, this is not always possible. As previously discussed, the commitments and responsibilities in our lives do not always allow it. What I suggest to many women with whom I have worked is that they create a healing sanctuary within their home, a special place and moment where they can sit within their own silence, looking at who they are and nurturing all aspects of themselves as a sacred woman. It is very important that you create this time when you feel that you absolutely need time alone to integrate what is taking place within you.

In this chapter we will create a healing sanctuary. Within this sanctuary you will further invoke the empowerment of the Complete Earthly Woman. You will activate your union within your heart and hand over all that you wish to surrender, to allow the true you to manifest within all aspects of your life. The following ritual is something you can do as many times as you feel necessary. However, you need only do it once properly to witness a shift within yourself. In the days following this ritual, look within yourself and see if you sense the presence of the Complete Earthly Woman guiding your way. Look for small coincidences—her sacred calling cards.

So how do you create this healing sanctuary in your life? Firstly, be honest with yourself. Accept that you need it and accept that you will discipline your life so that you can have the experience. In my home I rarely have time alone. I contribute to my husband's business, I have been writing this book daily for five years and I have two children. So time alone seems like a distant memory.

The most productive part of the day for me is to spend time on myself in the evening. No matter how exhausted I have been or how difficult it has seemed to find time for myself, I have achieved it. I know that the time to romance myself is vital.

The path of self-development is not designed to pull you away from your family and your commitments, even though at times it is difficult not to resent our responsibilities and the people in our lives who rely on us when we desperately seek time out. I can tell you from experience that you can effectively — without resentment and without abandoning your post — spend time on yourself. I have found that the best place in a busy life to find time out is in the bathroom, which can make a very beautiful sanctuary for self-healing.

How Do You See Your Healing Sanctuary?

From this point begin to visualize your perfect sanctuary, a place that nurtures your soul. Is it simple? Does it have flowers? Do you see soft candlelight and hear soft music? Is your bath overflowing with bubbles, and are you covered in a mudpack, inhaling yourself wholly, empowered and centered in the brilliance of unconditional love? Sound great? Well, I would think that you deserve this sacred experience, so allow yourself to have it.

Chapter 8

Preparing Your Sacred Room

Before you begin setting up your bathroom for your inner retreat you will need to clean it. Wash the bath, the floor and the benches, and put everything away. Take any dirty laundry from the room, and wash or remove any bathmats and replace them with clean towels.

To set up your bathroom you will need:

1 tape/CD player

1 tape/CD of relaxation music (must be instrumental)

1 pen

1 notebook for writing

Clean towels

7 white candles (large or small) & matches

1 bunch of freshly cut flowers

Aromatherapy burning oils or incense (optional)

A sign for the door "Please Do Not Disturb—Sanctuary of the Complete Earthly Woman"

1 set of sleepwear, freshly washed

1 pair of socks or slippers

1 bottle of body cream

1 sponge for washing

1 jar of Epsom salts

Bubble bath

1 rose quartz crystal (optional)

1 copy of *Complete Earthly Woman*

Lay out your room to nurture your soul:

Make the room up to feel right for you.

Put your flowers where you can see them, maybe even dress them up with big bows or something to make them more special than usual.

Place your notebook, pen and copy of *Complete Earthly Woman* next to the bath. Hang your sign on the door.

Pour your bubbles and oils in the bath.

Put your rose quartz crystal in the water (if you have a crystal; if not, they are very cheap and easy to find).

Place your candles in a circle around the room to create a circular glow around you. You can sit some on the edge of the bath, as long as you create the best circle that you can.

After you have prepared your room, filling and preparing your bath, light your candles, turn on the music and leave the room, closing the door behind you.

Sacred Bathroom Ritual—Invocation

Before going back into your room to have your time alone and connect to the Complete Earthly Woman you need to sit quietly and speak to your heart through the following conscious breathing invocation.

Begin by inhaling deeply into a vision of the Complete Earthly Woman, which is you. Envision your most empowered self smiling back at you. Ask your heart to provide you with an experience of love, that in this moment of this retreat you will release and purify aspects of your life and re-create your energy centers.

Inhale inner peace. Close your eyes and *inhale courage*, asking that in this bath you will merge into all aspects of yourself.

While continuing to inhale deeply, hold your arms forward for the Complete Earthly Woman and assure her that you are prepared and longing to merge within yourself. Continue to inhale deeply for a couple of minutes. Walk toward the healing sanctuary and enter the sacred healing light of the Complete Earthly Woman. Be aware through this entire process of each breath you take. Pace your experience to the rhythm of your breathing. Stay focused on inhaling the splendor of this transformation, and exhale all resistance from the thinking mind.

Upon entering your healing sanctuary:

When you enter the bathroom, inhale the magnificence and the glow of the golden light that fills the room.

Feel yourself relax as you inhale each breath deeply within.

Shut your door quietly and slowly.

Feel the magnificent presence that fills this room—how beautiful and nurturing is the feeling.

It is almost as if the feeling is caressing your skin through the glowing, golden light. Slowly, peacefully and sensually remove your clothes. Allow yourself in this private sanctuary to merge into your sensuality, into the golden light of sacred wisdom and healing. As you slowly undress, love yourself. Love your female presence and sweetness. Love who you uncover from your clothes. Love the moment of nurturing yourself in this way—this private, sacred self-worship.

After you have removed your clothes, walk to the mirror and look into it. Look at you. Within the mirror you see the temple of light that you are. Deeply inhale self-love and deeply exhale your immediate thoughts of resistance toward yourself as you look into the mirror at your naked body. Deeply inhale the golden light of the sacred inner woman and exhale all criticisms and judgments of who you are.

Consciously inhale the golden light of the room and continue to accept your radiant beauty as you peacefully look into the mirror.

As you watch your reflection, look into the center of your eyes. Breathe into the center of your eyes. Focus on your pupils. With each breath do not shift your stare; stay focused on your pupils and deeply inhale the golden light.

As you look into your eyes, remaining focused on your pupils and breathing, you feel yourself awaken from within your heart. Within your eyes you see the most captivating beauty appear. A radiant, glowing beauty is looking back at you. *Inhale this beauty, as you are this beauty.*

In this moment, in each breath, you have awakened an aspect of yourself that is pure love and pure divinity. Smile at yourself in the mirror. Smile into the reflection within your eyes. Finally you see yourself. Within the center of your eyes awaits your True self.

Your True self awaits to merge through your conscious participation in re-creating your life, to merge within your life and all aspects of your life through conscious breathing. Welcome this divine aspect of yourself into this moment, confirming within your heart your excitement to consciously participate in your own inner transformation. Smile courageously at yourself; invoke your determination through your admiration for your inner beauty.

Slowly turn away from the mirror still continuing to deeply inhale and peacefully exhale. Slowly get into the bath. Lie back into the bath and continue to breathe. Consciously inhale the golden light that circles you from your seven candles. Lie back and merge into the nurturing warmth of this sacred bath. As you lie with your eyes closed, stay in the vision of who you saw in your reflection in the mirror. Spend a few moments merging in the beauty of this moment by consciously inhaling the peace, the golden light and your vision.

As you relax, pick up your pen and notebook and write out the following:

> *As I lie here in this pool of healing light I merge within the inner beauty and self-empowerment of the Complete Earthly Woman. In contribution to this sacred union I release issues that cause me discomfort such as the time . . .*

Use this moment to let go of everything that you need to in order to be free within yourself—free to experience self-love. As you write this letter stay focused on every breath.

After completing this letter, empty your Epsom salts into your bath. Continue to lie in the warm water, peacefully relaxed. Continue to deeply inhale. Gently lie back in the bath. Inhale the following by repeating these invocations silently to yourself, and inhale as you hear your mind repeating what you say:

> *I invoke the presence of my empowered self.*
> *I am a Complete Earthly Woman.*

Repeat these two lines as many times as you can for twenty minutes.

After you have repeated these invocations, peacefully attuning to them with each breath, get out of the bath. Walk to the mirror and smile to yourself. No matter what you feel at this time, it is part of you discovering yourself. Simply know and accept that on this sacred day you nurtured your sacred self. After you have dressed, leave one candle burning. Take your letter and the candle into your garden or to a place where you can safely set fire to the letter. As you set fire to the letter inhale the invocation *I am an inner flame of purification* over and over until the letter has turned to ash and dissolved onto the ground.

I suggest to you that you have the experience of this sacred retreat as many times and as often as you feel. You may try consciously breathing some invocations from Chapter 3 in your sacred bath, which will also be a very empowering attunement to your heart.

This environment is the best place to begin each of the Complete Earthly Woman initiations in Chapter 11. Feel great about your achievement and allow yourself this sacred experience whenever you feel it is necessary for you to have time for re-creating you.

9.

Peace with the Past

Forgiveness

A vital step in claiming self-power is to first forgive your-self. Forgive yourself for the actions you took in your life that came from learned behavior. Like many of us, I had to forgive myself for misguided relationships, irrational behavior and addictions. I had to forgive myself for the manner in which I had abused the privilege of being a woman. By 1994 the betrayal of this abuse consumed me to my deepest depths of despair. I was on my knees in desperation. It was the first time that I experienced real fear of who I was. I remember lying on the floor in my home. It had been robbed the week before. I had nothing. They had taken my car, clothes, furniture, toiletries—everything. It was the third time that I had been robbed in four years, and I did not have the mental energy to fix the situation. I just chose to deny it. Literally, I was on the floor in exhausting nothingness. I felt as if a part of me was crawling around inside begging, screaming to get out. I remember that my grandmother phoned to see how I was. Always at the right time she would throw the life rope. She knew that I was in a very bad way. I told her that when I closed my eyes I saw a dark tunnel, that I was in the tunnel and I was afraid. Pushed to the brink by my state, she began to cry for me to get help. She said that she had the name of a psychiatrist who had written a new book on depression, and asked if I would see him if she could get me an appointment. Agreeing to this, we hung up.

Lying on the floor after our call I began to laugh, thinking of another psychiatrist telling me I was perfectly normal, that I was just having experiences of sadness. Of the many I had seen, none had uncovered my grief.

Only a short time after speaking with my grandma I received a phone call telling me that I had an appointment with the new psychiatrist. During my first visit I told him my story. A little person within peeked her head out and cried, "Help." He looked into my eyes and said, "You don't have to be afraid any longer. I will help you." Connecting to my pain, he stammered with tears.

This was the first day of rebuilding my self-worth. His reaction to my story said that I was worth the attention. Over the next three years of seeing this man we laughed, we cried—I was safe. My inner child loved him. He could see her pain. He heard her pain and he did the best he could to keep me going. I was on enough medication to hypnotize an elephant, and at the time it was perfect. It was as if I was on a mental vacation. My mind sat in silence, numb on prescribed drugs. They kept me alive. When I spent times on low doses I spoke to myself about improving my life. Then as quickly as I was up, I was down. Within what would seem like moments I would crash into a pit of depression. Up would go the medication and I was on "vacation" again. I had so much grief inside. It was not just the sexual abuse that created the depression; it was the mental, emotional and physical abuse set into play by other people in my life. These people had seemed to have joy in humiliating me, intimidating me and violating my free will. I was shattered. No part of my psyche was healthy.

I had spent twelve years saying to myself (especially throughout puberty), "What is wrong with me? Why do they laugh at me and ridicule me? I want to be loved. I am not a bad person, please someone love me—even for a moment." The medication stopped this repetitive chatter within my mind, which was seeking love. It put the victim to sleep, which at the time was exactly what saved me.

The turning point for me was when I awoke in a hospital. My first visit to the psychiatric ward. There I was in the line for medication, having just attempted to end my life for the seventh time. I was sitting numbed, in a self-help group, cutting and pasting Christmas cards. Looking into the eyes of others and seeing their pain and silently hoping for them that they would find love and cheer up. I stayed like this for five weeks. Then one day I said, "That's enough, no more!" I saw that it was the harshness and denial of others that put me into that hospital. As they refused to see my pain, so did I. My inner child, adolescent and every living aspect of myself was crying out for me to see myself—to own my pain. The worthlessness would only go when I was brave enough to love and honor myself. To cease laying blame and to take responsibility. I rang my psychiatrist and told him I was returning home. He gave me his blessing and increased my medication, and I was off home. During our next visit he told me that I should move away. He explained to me that even though I had my moments in which I was unaware of life, I also had moments of being deeply connected with my healing process. He suggested to me as a friend that if I moved away, then maybe I could break patterns and cycles of behavior, simply by not being in the face of certain members of my family and others in my life. He said that being alone might help me get in touch with myself and empower me to stop living as a victim of the actions and expectations of others.

The main problem in my life that had caused me to mentally fall was that I had expected my family to treasure me. When some had not, I had resented them. The anger that I had was insurmountable. They sensed this anger and resented it. This caused our relationship to struggle along even more. My psychiatrist suggested that if I moved he would refer me to another doctor, one who would support me in the same way that he had. So I did it. Within days I moved to another state, sunny Queensland in Australia. Financially, physically, mentally and emotionally my life was a huge mess. It took the greatest courage to walk away from my doctor, who had become a true friend, and leave behind the safety net that he had provided for me. However, I wanted to have the experience of courage. I wanted to be faced with the challenge of having to change and having to look after myself and to be strong.

When I arrived at my destination I could not believe the freedom I saw in people, their joy, the beach, the sun. All of a sudden I experienced me as an adult, responsible for myself. Not waiting for an abusive visit or phone call from anyone in my family. I could not feel their negative thoughts toward me. The courage that it took for me to leave seemed to empower and protect me in some way. I was shaking but standing. This is when I realized that my medication had helped me by providing a mental rest. However, it was also denying me the process of finding myself, so I began to look for ways to replace the medication with healthy alternatives.

I took herbs, I wrote, I walked, and I ate a healthy diet. I refused all contact with anyone in my family who wanted to put me down. I began setting healthy boundaries in my life, defining what was good for me and what was not. Under the supervision of my psychiatrist over the phone, within six months I was off the medication. I was depressed, but nothing like before. I was afraid, and yet I was determined to be me, determined to experience myself outside of the labels and baggage and interpretations of others. It was as if at the time my inner mantra was: *I want to be me. I am not this grief. I want to be me.* As I changed, the people who appeared in my life were different. They were not stricken with grief. They openly saw my pain, and they openly made suggestions on how to change. Suddenly I could feel life taking a different turn. Within months I had turned my life around.

The most important step I took at this time was forgiveness. Forgiveness for myself. I had been my worst critic, continually putting myself down for how I was coping and the direction I was taking. Then at the moment of this transition of moving away, I looked back to who I was when around my family. I smiled at myself for my behavior toward myself and others. I began to see my behavior as a child's behavior. I realized that I had behaved the best that I could, as we can only ever be who we are shown to be. This realization allowed me to forgive myself. This forgiveness opened my door to the desire to both improve and increase the value of my life. It ignited my flame of purification, lighting it with one incredible experience.

Letting Go

You will see by now that within this life I have chosen experiences that have taken both trust and discipline to master. What seemed to be the most destructive experiences took place at significant developmental stages of my childhood and adolescence, thus evolving and establishing foundations of negative emotional, mental and physical programming throughout my entire subconscious mind. Today I know that the shattering pain that I was experiencing within has been re-created because my life and level of joy and understanding is my measure. In comparison to yesterday, today is a conscious day.

I give to you in this moment the truth from within my own transformation—this opening of the heart. I invite you to commit to the magnificence of diving within yourself, knowing that you are divine. You are truthful purity and an empowered heart. Whatever your circumstances, let go to the wisdom that we are all equal, and in being here we have the opportunity to obtain complete, whole transformation. How? Through faith, through the acceptance that you are, and your life is, the essence of transformation. As much as Mother Earth transforms within the harmony of nature, so can you.

Faith is knowing that you are worth it. No person is more or less worthy than another; rather, our experiences simply set up our interpretations of worthiness based on how we participate in our lives. If you choose to dive within the peaceful pool of life within yourself and go beyond your circumstances you will know that we are all worthiness.

Where I Find True Self

To obtain your True self you must go within. Locating the strength and courage to do this is simple. All you need to do is vow to your heart that you will honor all with whom you travel along your path with truth. What is it to honor another in this way—with truth? It is to establish the boundaries that invite others into your life, into your experience as carriers of truth, love and integrity. If you establish this foundation—that a person who does not honor your space with these values cannot be part of your life—then you are honoring all of life with truth. The truth in setting this boundary is that you only accept right conduct into your life, no matter who the person or what the experience. Living your life this way allows your True self to live comfortably in all of your experiences. It is not that your True self is not present throughout your whole life; it is. However, the clearer and more purified your life and your mind, the more the True self can operate throughout life as a peaceful, wise divinity, delivering the message of inner joy and not the plea to transform. You will know when you have created your life to honor your True self, because your life and your experiences will reflect the purity and unconditional love of your True self.

Honoring Another

It is also vital to use these values in dealing with all people and experiences in your life. Whether a person is in your life five minutes or five years, you should relate to that person with integrity, peace and kindness. To fully transform your sacred space to one of peace and truth you must share with others only peace and truth. These two values are the values of love. These values are actually the experience of unconditional love.

Peace guides us into understanding one another. Through peace we hear the inner voice within the heart, the voice that speaks the simplicity of kindness. It is not the voice that speaks the complication of judgment, or the voice analyzing another's faults, but the voice that simply decides to give love silently. If we truly respect ourselves we have the capacity to respect others. By respecting ourselves it becomes easy to remain peaceful about another person and send all situations love. We should only ever worry how we behave, not how others behave.

If you are dissatisfied with a situation, you have the choice to walk away. If it is not the right time to walk away then have faith, locate your worthiness and know that one day you will be freed of such behavior. Speak to the inner light within; seek guidance on how to move on. Agree within yourself that you accept the experience as a lesson and the person as a teacher. Then accept the situation as showing you who you are by asking you what you are prepared to accept as your Truth. Make the decision and accept or ask to move on.

Sometimes we face painful situations and we never have the choice to move on. This creates great disharmony within us. To send the person or the experience love at times seems both ridiculous and difficult; however, it is again very simple. The best love you can give another is not to mentally say, "Yes, I forgive, and you are my teacher." This is unrealistic, because if a situation was bad enough, it is quite possible that you will not mean it. So the best and most effective way to deal with this situation is to forgive yourself for your reaction, for your guilt or for whatever interpretations you made of the experience. After this, repeat over and over to your heart that the person or experience may receive the love that shines in abundance from Mother Earth. Ask that they inhale her essence of self-transformation. Inhale as you repeat this to yourself, and inhale Mother Earth's essence for them. Taking this action after any situation that has created pain in your life is the action of humility.

When you demonstrate humility for your experiences and the spiritual lessons behind them you will catapult along the path of self-discovery.

Accepting Your Inner Knowing

You will be identifying with a deep aspect of your inner consciousness when you tune into the level of inner knowing that encourages you to accept that you are able to learn in every situation. Your inner knowing is your inner voice that you respond to as, "I knew this was going to be the outcome," or "I had a feeling this could be the outcome." Accepting this voice and the guidance that is given is the first initiation on the path of the Complete Earthly Woman. It is when you say, "I trust in this inner guidance. I know that I am more than what is seen on the outside." It is making the conscious choice to come together, to follow this inner voice and surrender to truth. It is the process of recovering self-worth, of knowing that you are the action of the divine wisdom that speaks within. It is when you will begin to see the mind as a child that knows no better than its interpretations, which can be fear, betrayal, frustration or victimization.

I found accepting my life became easier and seemed to accelerate rapidly along the path of self-development when I accepted that life is a spiritual play. We all have our part to play, and this is what we do. In accepting this I was able to accept all of what had taken place. I finally moved to the understanding that my gifts had come from my worst violators. I call them violators for the purpose of this moment, because in the repercussions of their actions my mind felt violated. However, the experiences they gave me are writing this book and opening my heart.

The experiences they gave me have opened the floodgates of love—self-love—turning the experiences in which I have felt most violated into the most empowering gifts of self-transformation. The acute sadness that I experienced with my parents took me directly within. In doing so I have opened my heart to the experience of true love. Nothing can beat it.

Today I have two beautiful children and a loving husband. He is my best friend and most aligned spiritual companion to the experience of my heart. My capacity to love these souls is overwhelming, considering that my mind was not educated in the practice of love based on my life's experiences. Locating this love was both needed and vital. In the experience of self-love today, I can truly love these souls unconditionally, consciously surrendering to nurture every part of them. Striving with discipline to master loving them as I master loving myself, in the capacity of pure unconditional love.

Hearing and following the call within to nurture myself by healing the mind and aligning to the heart is a gift. My life and my varied—almost nightmarish—experiences have given me a fulfilling life. Through this knowing I invite you to go within your experiences and locate your channel of unconditional love. Ask the heart for one answer to one question to carry you forward, and it will give you ten answers and carry you ten steps. That is the beauty of inner knowing, which can be seen as self-love.

Giving Each Situation Unconditional Love

If you look back into different experiences and go within your emotional, mental and physical reactions to each experience, you may find it unrealistic that you give love to a situation or an individual.

This is both normal and acceptable at the beginning of your self-transformation. Giving love to each situation does not mean the mind agrees that the situation that emotionally tortured you is acceptable. It means that you honor your participation based on what you learned from the experience.

Giving love to a situation can be accomplished through visualizing color, self-invocation and conscious breathing. This is how I did it. Very rarely was I able to sit silently and repeat to myself and say to my heart, "Thanks for the sexual abuse and mental denigration, what a benefit." Forget it. I had to sit silently and address my pain during breathing. As I breathed I repeated things like, "I let go in love." In my mind I would see the person, try to feel the experience and breathe. Then I would see the color pink fill me and surround them. That simple. No mental analysis. Just goodbye fear, hello spiritual Truth.

At times I go back within my mind to the experiences in my life during which my mind suffered acute pain. I smile triumphantly at how I live today. I know that I am purity, and I experience this purity within my heart and mind every day. I dissolved the fear of sharing this purity, and now I protect it with integrity. When I was first introduced to my purest self I hid away, afraid that life's responsibilities and the flow of life would remove me from my purity and I would lose it. Today, however, I have identified that as a whole person I am purity. I discovered that to seek this purity and transformation within myself and to remain disciplined is a silent gift that emerged from within. I discovered that it is a gift that I wanted to feel this aspect of myself, that I wanted this life for myself. I wanted the baggage to go.

I heard a calling to let go within myself, so I went for it, asking over and over to myself for self-transformation, refusing to fall down in a heap or to fail in succeeding to overcome the pain.

The Female Warrior

I come across many female victims. I know them, because I have lived as one. Why are there victims? There are no victims in the land of universal Truth—only female warriors. What is a female warrior? She is persistent in finding herself and sharing her love. She is not masculine, and she is not afraid. She is not beating up on herself with hang-ups and grief about who she is. She knows who she is. Everything she faces is a victory. Everyone she nurtures blossoms within their hearts. She is giving of the wisest wisdom and the most courageous courage.

As a woman the female warrior is soft. She is the fire of sexuality and the humility of a precious heart. She is everything that nurtures humanity. She is who you are in your truest form, connected to the heartbeat of Mother Earth, living as the ancient heartbeat of sacred Truth. She is the aspect of yourself that you bring through while practicing and becoming part of what is written here, through slowly looking within and making friends with your most divine aspect. It is in making friends with the divine aspect that your mind will be nurtured and excited at your newly found beauty. This inner beauty is the essence of the female warrior, the one you shine to be—as you re-create the one you thought yourself to be into the one you know yourself to be.

Your Own Master

Once you have identified with how you treat yourself as a woman, it is vital to love all of your behavior. Accept that you are your own master and that all of your experiences are teaching you to perfect self-mastery. Smile at who you are, and feel compassion within your heart for yourself. Accept your life, accept your choices and, most importantly, accept that the various relationships that move in and out of your life are your most empowering teachers along the path of self-love. Relationships show us who we are. If you want to master peace within your relationships, do it with conscious breathing. Be responsible for living your life. Own your behavior and re-create your interpretations through conscious breathing. Replace your interpretations by consciously inhaling the seven invocations—Peace with Your Past. Slowly but surely you will meet and become self-mastery through the action of forgiveness and acceptance.

Allowing the Beauty of Love

Today I can say that the glue to my wholeness is the honor I have in joining my journey with a true whole male. A strong, courageous, wise man who has been fearless in identifying and releasing his programming within the negative ego. It has been pure beauty and honor to watch him merge with his female side and balance his masculine and feminine aspects in the truth that women are sacred love. In service and love I give wholly to my partner.

In the experience of unconditionally loving him I know that I have forgiven and I have identified with my past because I am truly in love with a *man*. I honor his love and I trust him completely with every aspect of my life.

What made this love? Spiritual Truth allowed us to come together. When you attain peace with your past, self-love will shine within your heart. You will attract a huge capacity of love from another through the experience of seeking to love yourself. It will happen through locating your unconditional love on the inside, and as a result you will receive unconditional love on the outside. This will balance your life to be a whole experience of pure love, all by attaining peace with your past. So give to yourself this gift — the worthiness to receive love through the action of knowing that you are love and experiencing peace with your past.

Capacity to Love

What is love?
It is complete acceptance of who you are.
It is knowing true love through knowing you.
It is using this self-love as a message to love others,
as in loving yourself you say,
I can love you
because I love myself.
I honor you
because I honor myself.
I accept you
because I accept myself.
Together in the experience of love,
the expression of self-love,
we merge into the inner outer union of unconditional love.

I share with you at this point the divine brilliance and experience of unconditional love. It is the love that I share with two beautiful children and my true soul companion, my husband. I share with you this love at this moment to both encourage and empower you to create the same environment of love through your transformation to self-love. It is through merging within your self-love that you will invoke unconditional love from those around you.

Two Beautiful Gifts

What beautiful gifts I have received in the last four years! Two beautiful children, two of my teachers of higher understanding. Our children never miss the opportunity to tidy up our actions or teach us to identify with our intentions. At times I am overcome as I witness their souls and experience their unconditional love passing in and out of my heart.

Since I carried our daughter for nine months I have referred to her as the "medicine woman." At times she seems completely aware of how she triggers our self-awareness to look at our behavior. She has both tamed my ego and healed my self-hatred, an aspect of the personality that has taken constant attention from me over the last four years.

I remember a day — an incredible step for me on this journey. One day I looked into my daughter's eyes; she was almost three years old. When our eyes connected I saw her face for the first time. I saw her beauty and her vulnerability and heard her precious voice.

I saw her confusion. As much as I adored her, our relationship had lacked a whole connection, because in living with her innocence and her child I experienced the process of self-hatred within my inner child. The little girl within me seemed to resent my daughter to some degree, because I was putting so much effort into my daughter, which caused my precious little girl within to again feel rejected in her life. Through this action of the inner child I could not fully connect to my daughter's soul. It was not that I failed to truly see her. I was afraid of her innocence and vulnerability, as I had failed to identify with my own. In my life my inner child had lost her innocence and vulnerability through abuse. She very hesitantly made friends with my baby daughter. In resistance to the responsibility of this little girl she put up a shield of self-hatred that said, "There is too much fear in here to let you in. Why are you here, and why do we have to look after you? What about me?"

It was on this beautiful day that my daughter and I connected within the heart. The shield melted away and I felt and saw her for the first time.

My inner child felt safe with this precious little girl, and slowly they are becoming the best of friends. Such a blessed "medicine woman" is this precious girl, joining us on this sacred journey and filling our hearts with unconditional love. She has assisted me in healing my most important alignment to the Complete Earthly Woman—my inner child and my self-hatred. I am so honored to be sharing such an incredible exchange of soul love and wisdom with this precious soul. Warming my heart, expanding my consciousness and nurturing my soul are all gifts from you, princess—thank you.

She has taught me to seek love, and in doing so I can abundantly exchange love with her in our individual roles. My childhood was never an example for raising my own children.

The strength and commitment to honor them and assist them with integrity, honesty and good example comes from the determination and divine wisdom within my heart. I look for myself in them. I look to heal all of myself in their purity and vulnerability. In doing this I can nurture their lives, their choices and their hearts.

The opening of my heart came from our little boy—our beloved. A little old man on a big mission, in awe of his sister and further training his parents in self-mastery of unconditional love. He arrived in our arms and swept us into the chambers of higher consciousness. His sister worked us over, preparing us to love this precious soul that radiates pure love of the heart.

I connected with him immediately when he arrived. The love I have for this little boy has exploded my heart, and sacred wisdom has flowed forth from the most divine aspect, opening a heart that still felt fear of experiencing love. This little boy has looked at me through the eyes of divinity and bestowed me with love; this I have both seen and experienced. He opens the channel of honor and humility, and such tenderness and grace of God is now part of this sacred journey. The love they have bestowed is love of complete appreciation. I feel both honored and complete as a woman since they have arrived in our lives.

So our two beautiful children—soul mates—have joined me and healed me in a sacred exchange of love. As a mother in admiration of their spiritual energy I look at their innocence in giving us their grace. I see and feel my inner child happy and drawing in the love that comes from these two precious souls.

Until this turning point in my life I had not experienced a connection with young children, nor did I want to. It was not on my agenda to have children in the state that I was in. However, miracle after miracle bought them into my life, and then miracle after miracle bought us together in an exchange of sacred love. Their divine innocence has been my inspiration to merge within my capacity to give and receive love. I am determined through devotion and love to honor their spiritual journey and all aspects of their lives, abundantly filling their hearts and nurturing their souls.

I thank them every day for the love which has blossomed from the purity within my heart, an aspect I have never before experienced—a dream come true. Their love is unconditional, and that to me is the greatest gift one can ever receive.

It is important to consciously strive to be your best when you are responsible for such innocence as that of children. This is not to say that your life must be completely healed and you perfectly balanced. It is to accept that their existence is what both empowers and accelerates your growth. See how I have taken an experience such as that of my daughter and pursued the highest teaching within the situation. The highest teaching is identified in a positive way that will affect and be received by the subconscious mind as positive soul growth. It is education to the subconscious mind for both of us.

With this situation I could have felt negative about what had taken place and headed on the path of guilt. But I went the path of love. All of us receive love and learning if we are open to our own contribution to the situation. To reach higher understanding in the experience with my daughter, I spoke to her soul.

I asked her to come through some way and show me where she was. When the time was right I had the self-realization of truth and identified with the blockages in our relationship.

When we begin seeking these realizations in everything,
we begin riding the rapids of self-realizations.
As we move our thoughts to a positive vibration,
the flow of self-realizations becomes calm and constant.
Life becomes a continuous flow of self-realizations.

The next master in taking me into my capacity to love is

my beloved husband, the gold embossed clause within the spiritual contract. The precious man with whom I circled the sun in my sacred dream. For three and a half years the rock pool of tranquility sat within my heart, vibrating the essence of an empowering love. Now that love is here, and I am deeply committed and residing within my heart in the oneness of love with this precious soul.

The connection of what I am experiencing is the crème de la crème of spiritual partnerships. In every single aspect of who we are, we are constantly mirroring one another's highest truth, in a magnified "do not slip" manner. Ours is a relationship teaching self-mastery and humility. The capacity to love this precious soul has been a challenge to cultivate, because I was so overwhelmed to receive such a divine jewel of love within my life that it took my breath away for a year and a half. Then I began to breathe, and I saw him. Our precious children joined us and here we are, an experience of love—divine love.

My husband and I did not initially fall head over heals in love with one another. We felt a connection, and we made it work by disciplining our minds and the expectations we had of one another. We agreed to find ourselves, and in that process we found each other, hearts open and completely nurturing each other's soul.

To further empower this experience of unconditional love for one another, we are very disciplined in our actions and intentions toward one another. We always try to guide the other with love and not criticism. We nurture one another's antics and transformation through compassion and inclusion in one another's process. I have a passionate nature, and he works very hard to respect this quality. He knows and appreciates how I will respond, excited and involved with everything. He has also overcome childhood trauma and transformed his thinking mind into an expression of highest teachings. He resides within his heart and offers both integrity and honor to all passing through his life. If there is one action I have learned from him, it is the action of honor.

Honor and Love

In coming together with my husband I have found myself to honor his radiant male role in a manner that has been previously foreign to me. I love looking after him and nurturing him. I love to understand him and at times hold his hand and warm his heart. I love it when I see his inner child peek out and say hello to our children, or look to me for a special treat and a hug. The child within is a strong influence in my husband's life.

As my husband's closest companion I watch him move in and out of experiences in his life, and I always open myself to his experiences. This way I know when he needs to be nurtured by the mother aspect—the ancient vibration of Mother Earth that exists within my womb. In being aware of his spiritual needs I am able to allow the Complete Earthly Woman to nurture him and also transform his thinking mind and empower his radiant heart. I have witnessed in my husband (and in men I have counseled on a professional level) that for a man to live within his heart and open his female aspect in harmony, he must have an environment of unconditional love. If he is in a relationship, then the relationship must be warm and cozy.

In my relationship with my husband we openly share commitment and love. It is easy to become disassociated from what will truly benefit your partner. Life can become so busy and commitments so many, but you must give priority to your loved ones first. When you give an abundance of love to another, it will only help you, as long as that love is humbly received and appreciated. If you can help your partner to merge within the heart, then your partner will help you merge within yours through unconditional love. I know within my heart that my husband has given me something very, very special within my heart because the love, honor, humility and respect I have for every aspect of his entire life is abundant.

The measure of this love does not say that we have always been on a course of smooth sailing. We have struggled at times, gasping for breath to find ourselves amongst the duty and responsibility to our children and one another. However, through working as a team to nurture the whole person of one another, we have reached the point of unconditional love with one another. This is an experience of abundant joy and true companionship.

Throughout my life, until meeting my husband, I failed to love others in a healthy, balanced way. I either yearned for the wrong type of love or demonstrated the wrong type of love: mental love, unable-to-connect-to-the-heart love. Within this transformation of giving love is also the beauty in being able to accept love.

Today I am unceasingly surrounded in love. It does not always come packaged in a big red bow of acceptance. It may come as a lesson—simply a blessing of awareness and realization of how I may better myself. I feel constantly surrounded in love, because I am constantly focused on giving and receiving love in all situations. I feel that it is important to identify with the love that exists within me today, because it is an accomplishment of my inner determination. The conditioning and behavior programming of my life had locked shut the gates of love. To open those gates, I first had to walk toward them. The gates of love open the more that you grow and mature along the path of self-awareness, consciously re-creating your expectations and actions of love through conscious breathing.

Creating Harmony Within Your Relationship/Yourself

From the love I experience with my husband and the issues that we have faced together, I can honestly tell you that it is vital in a relationship to have no expectations of the future or the ability for one another to change. Don't lock each other in a box by saying, "You are this way, and I am stuck with it. You'll never change," etc.

This type of behavior is not only detrimental to the growth of the soul but also to the future of your relationship and the growth within yourself, because you are choking the other person of their growth and their experience. I remember my stepfather used to say, "You can't change the spots on a leopard," and then one day I read a quote in a spiritual book that said, "Through invoking the action of highest teachings and the knowing that we are all one, you can change the spots on leopard, because I am the leopard and I am the spots."

Commitment to your partner will come from commitment to yourself. When you strive for happiness within yourself you strive to make another happy. In making them happy they make you happy. Then the circle of unconditional love bonds around your lives and fills your heart. When the bond grows stronger the commitment flourishes into a magnificent rose of love. The pure beauty and sweet essence that comes from this rose is inhaled by all who come into your presence. Through inhaling this beauty they ask one question: "What is the beauty that I sense here?" As a couple, committed and in the experience of love, you smile and comment, "You inhale the beauty of self-love, unconditional love, our love."

When I work with various couples today and with women seeking relationships I continually explain to them that love is simple and abundant. It is created as a reflection of who you are and where you are in your life. To really experience true, earthly, whole, complete love you must love yourself. Nurture yourself and be courageous in accepting who you are so you can share that truth—the truth of who you are with another, safely and in trust. Seeking love when you are not experiencing this within yourself will only deliver a messenger of what you need to change.

So I say to you that there are two steps in healing your capacity to love and to receive love, initially within yourself and then within your life. The first step can be taken if you are alone and seeking true love, afraid that you will be alone forever. Let me say that if you feel alone, you are not ready to experience true love, because when you are in love with yourself you are the complete opposite of alone. Your life is filled with your creative character and childlike curiosity for life. You have fun finding yourself, nurtured by your own company. Time that we spend alone is vital and an integral part of learning who we are. Use it wisely. It is a gift in transforming your life. It is not to be feared but appreciated, for it is in this time that we can create our lives to be a reflection of our empowered heart and abundant inner truth. When you successfully do this alone, you will then find this with another.

The second step is if you are in an established relationship and wish to transform this relationship into an empowering experience of love. In this situation you need to first deal with yourself as an individual. Accept who you are as both duty to yourself and your duty to provide unconditional love and no judgment within your relationship. Come together through speaking about what love truly is, and nurture each other's descriptions. Make a conscious effort every day to create what the other sees as unconditional love, if these efforts are acceptable to your boundaries and healthy for the other person to receive as love. In relationships we participate in filling the hearts of one another. We learn humility, and through this humility and respect for the other person we find ourselves.

Empowering your own connection to your own heart is quickly achievable in a relationship if you are willing to use how you relate to your partner as another discipline that tells you how you relate to yourself.

From experience I tell you that no matter where you have traveled in your life and no matter what challenges come up in your relationship, if you find love within, the universe will provide love to wholly complete your life. I am so thankful to myself for my courage, discipline and determination to find myself, to find my True self and to become the best I can. In re-creating the circumstances of my life I have filled my life with love. I am so thankful for this love. I am so thankful for the universe overflowing my capacity to both give and receive love. In finding love I threw a boomerang that asked the questions, "Who am I? Where will I find love?" Not long afterward I caught that boomerang, and it was solid gold. It said, "Hello, I am love. The key to your heart. Open your eyes. In seeing yourself, you see love. Welcome to your capacity to love. I return, both within your heart and within your life, your truly empowered self: Complete Earthly Woman."

Again I remind you that through the act of conscious breathing and self-awareness you can transform your capacity to give and receive love, undoubtedly transforming your life for the rest of your life. So do it. Spoil yourself. Today I am the queen of "spoil yourself"—abundantly spoiling myself with self-love and conscious knowing of my divinity in being a woman. In being a partner who is loved and nurtured through the action of self-love and self-nurturing. In living as a mother and a partner who is nurtured through the action of unconditional love and the commitment of self-transformation.

Sacred Initiations of the Complete Earthly Woman

The following seven sacred initiations are your step-by-step journey within—your gift to becoming your truly empowered self. You will make conscious choices throughout the following initiations and take action to become a Complete Earthly Woman. These initiations are gifts of love to all women. Through your own transformation you will become an instrument of change for Mother Earth. In the action of your sacred transformation an abundant flow of goodness is filtered into Mother Earth, re-creating the world to become a more harmonious residence of unconditional love and the expression of highest teachings.

These initiations are sacred steps along the path to self-empowerment, and I suggest to you to believe, trust, and in faith, finish them. Opening the heart to your most empowered truth is going to be the most rewarding step you will ever take for your own personal development in your life. Completing them will bring overwhelming harmony into your life. These initiations are a safe progression along the path of self-empowerment. Within these initiations is the freedom to make the sacred transformation at the speed that suits your capacity to change. This is a gift that will empower you to see it through until the end.

Miracles will happen once you begin this sacred transformation, and the essence of the Complete Earthly Woman will be all around you providing tools, experiences and an abundance of love to empower your transformation.

I implore you at this point to give yourself the gift of this sacred union within your heart. All resources such as courage, wisdom and discipline are abundant resources within that will flow as a river of transformation within your mind, emotions and body to carry you and walk with you to the final union with this sacred aspect of the woman, that which you are. I wish you abundant success!

To begin initiations 2–7 you will need to choose seven invocations from Chapter 3 for each specific initiation. These invocations are the essence of what you will become through inhaling what you wish to transform. To do this, read through the initiation. See how you will transform, and then ask yourself what you must change within yourself to make that transformation. See your weaknesses. Are they issues of sexuality, self-worth, physical appearances or relationships? Then read through and see which individual or group of invocations will remove your issues through attuning to the higher aspect within and allow you to completely heal and transform within the particular initiation. Follow your heart and the guidance that comes from it.

Tips

Each letter that you write to the Complete Earthly Woman eventually will have to be burned and thrown in the garden, invoking the act of creating new life. You may keep your writings until you feel that it is time that they go. You may even keep them until you have finished all seven initiations.

The choice is yours. However, eventually you should burn them.

Enjoy the process of each initiation and constantly remind yourself that you are experiencing an abundant gift of self-love. Let go and enjoy.

Keep your practice private. Leave your experiences—all of them—within your heart until you have completed each initiation, because we never know how another is going to relate to our experiences. Rather than receive negative suggestions about your experience and what you are doing, keep it to yourself until you have safely made the inner transformation.

 ## Initiation 1
Seek and Ye Shall Find

The first initiation is the step that is taken to find one's inner truth. It is the day that we first ask, "Who am I, truly?" Something within us aches to be free. We want to let go, to fill our hearts with unconditional love. Where else to find that love but within? This initiation allows us to accept that there is a Supreme Consciousness upon this planet. It can be referred to as God, Holy Spirit, Universal Source—whatever name is appropriate for both your religion and your inner vision of this sacred energy. This initiation is the moment in which you will seek the inner connection to this Supreme Consciousness within your heart. At the time of participating in this sacred initiation you are sitting in the palm of trans-formation. Be ready to let go and become.

Purpose: This sacred initiation is the moment in which you will assign your life, yourself and all in your life to this Supreme Intelligence for healing, purification and the essence of unconditional love. Invoking this initiation is the act of accepting that you are a magnificent light within. This is the time to believe it, believe it, believe it. Until you surrender to either wanting to believe in this sacred energy or knowing it exists, this initiation cannot be realized. The soul purpose of this initiation is to open the chamber of Truth within and to awaken the moment in which your life purpose is to seek your True self.

The Act of Invocation: When you invoke this initiation you may write a sacred letter to this Supreme Intelligence outlining your *commitment* and *belief* in connecting to the divine Truth within your heart. Write your commitment to honor all sacred aspects of the Complete Earthly Woman that manifest themselves in your life from the sacred chamber of light within your heart. Write a letter that connects to the self-belief that exists deep within your heart. Let go—within this letter—all your fear of transformation. Speak on paper of all you want to change in your life: how you see love, what is the ultimate gift that you can provide for humanity. Place this letter in a sacred place, as it is the beginning of the most sacred and powerful journey you will ever take: the self-discovery of you— your most divine, pure, calm, knowing, loving, joyful aspect. It is the most sacred letter that you will ever write in your life, a commitment to truth and unconditional love.

This sacred initiation will be complete when you feel the synchronicity of this connection of guidance within your life. You will begin to experience circumstances of coincidence and will be aware that you are having an intuitive experience about what's happening in your life. You will feel a stirring of companionship within your body. You will see changes in how you feel about yourself. Just be prepared and accepting of all spontaneous action around you. This initiation and your alignment to it will only appear as gentle love. Only love is what you will feel, excitement that you are being truly guided. This does not mean that from now on every situation in your life will become satisfying to the mind. It means that in all situations in your life you will be nurtured and educated by the heart to accept all situations through the actions of highest teachings. You will move in and out of your experiences, comforted by your inner connection. You will inherit the sacred understanding and universal law of your closest female companion—Mother Earth.

You will know that it is time for the next initiation when you are empowered and comforted within to take the next step. It will feel like a natural flow of growth.

ॐ ॐ ॐ

 **Initiation 2
I Love Myself**

Within this initiation is the magnificent gift of *inner strength.* Through owning our pain, our confusion and our roles in life we are empowered through inner strength and the beauty of acceptance. You are encouraged to meet yourself, complete and whole. You can do this through conscious breathing and working with different groups of invocations provided in Chapter 3. This is the initiation that is provided to let go of every single aspect of your inner and outer life that brings you down, that removes you from your empowered self.

Purpose: This is the initiation that will empower all acceptance of who you are and what is to change. As well as practicing seven invocations that you have chosen from Chapter 3, you will need to write many letters to the Supreme Intelligence of what you feel within and what you feel about yourself. Bring out tears, joy, fears, dreams in which you want to heal. Bring out that of which you want to be free. Let go— through your words—of relationships, experiences, expectations and fears of change. I wrote letter after letter after letter letting go of everything, leaving no stone unturned. I wrote out every single detail of what I felt needed to be removed so I could truly live in my heart. I wrote whenever I needed to write. I did not sit down in an organized, preplanned, daily manner. I wrote when I felt clouded by emotion, undisciplined racing thoughts or physical discomfort. I tried to write in the experience of the feeling.

I usually found that after surrendering how I felt in words to the Complete Earthly Woman within that I experienced an upliftment. Suddenly I became clear, and at times excited for myself, through my experience.

The Act of Invocation: The key to the success of this initiation is in your self-belief. You must truly believe that you are worthy to invoke such a powerful transformation in your life. In believing in yourself and your worthiness, unleash your determination. Stick to it no matter what. You will have asked for a lot; be prepared to give a lot by believing in yourself and by identifying what tests that belief. Have faith that this Supreme Universal Intelligence is absolutely devoted to bringing to life everything for which you ask.

You will know that this initiation is complete when you understand your life with a significant difference. An understanding and acceptance of life will be present within your life, your thoughts, your words, and your actions. You will have moments of excitement about who you are. At this point you will feel empowered and comforted to take the next step. It will be a natural flow of growth.

 Initiation 3
The Physical Invocation

The third initiation is invoking perfect *physical harmony*. Let go of all actions that harm and take the physical body out of perfect spiritual harmony. This is the initiation to let go of all addictions, food issues and physical expectations or to re-create sexual boundaries. It also serves to remove all conditioning—inherent and otherwise—within the cellular structure and memory of the body.

Purpose: Within the action of this sacred initiation you will identify with all aspects of your mind and emotions that are present in the energy of your body. You will identify with physical issues such as weight, health and well-being. You will connect with the body and synchronize your physical body, your thinking mind and your emotions. Within this initiation is the ability to balance hormones and re-create cellular memory on deep levels of programming.

The Act of Invocation: To invoke this initiation you must write a letter to the Supreme Consciousness outlining what you see as the best uses of the physical body. Write that you wish to use the physical body as a sacred temple, committing to Supreme Consciousness that in becoming your physical temple of light you will honor it as just that.

Commit that all sacred experiences and all unconditional love will be protected through right action. Commit that the sacred goddess that exists within will be protected through your direct demonstration of physical boundaries with others to honor your sacred role as a woman. This is the initiation through which you will stop seeking love in all the wrong places and start seeking love within. You will honor your body as a sacred temple through the act of good food, good thoughts and an active lifestyle. This is a time to "buff and scrub" the temple of light that houses the heart of soul truth.

After writing your letter of commitment to honor your temple of light, choose seven invocations that heal specific physical issues of which you wish to let go. These will generally be self-esteem issues, guilt or anger issues—specific behavior patterns that strongly affect the well-being of the physical body.

This initiation will be complete when you see and feel it. This can be a challenging initiation for some, not for all. The reason is that the physical body can be a storehouse of issues, so be prepared for some long, deep breaths. Be determined not to give up. At this point you will feel empowered to take the next step; it will be a natural flow of growth.

∾   ∾   ∾

Initiation 4
I Allow Change to Flow as a River of Wisdom

The fourth initiation is the invitation to allow *change* to flow through your life. It is the commitment to accept all change that will come about based on the changes that you make within yourself.

Purpose: This initiation will be the instrument that will encourage you to let go and have faith that all experiences are perfect for your growth. It is the invocation of letting go to the Supreme Consciousness and allowing the truth within your heart to change your life to accommodate the union with the Complete Earthly Woman.

The Act of Invocation: To invoke this sacred initiation, simply write a letter to the Supreme Consciousness inviting the action of change. In this letter ask for abundant love to empower your ability to accept change. When the changes begin to happen, let go of expectations, attachments and end results and allow changes to flow to completion.

You will also need to choose a group of invocations or seven individual invocations that define what you wish to change and practice them to further empower the changes that will take place. If you feel you should change your invocations, then do so at any time.

Watching these changes is empowering, comforting and miraculous. Invoke change, and it will remove you from self-doubt, misery and confusion and take you to joy, self-empowerment and your True self—the abundant love within your heart.

You will know this initiation is complete when changes in your life have occurred and you are empowered and peaceful with the changes. Identify with the highest teachings of experiencing these changes.

This is an initiation that you will carry you as a leading inner strength into all other initiations. At this point you will feel empowered and comforted to take the next step. It will be a natural flow of growth.

Initiation 5
I Invoke the Action of my Heart

This initiation lets you accept the person you are becoming and step within the heart.

Purpose: This can be the most emotional initiation and the one that might require a comfortable bed on which you can cry. This is the one where we bravely say "come on, let me have it" to the grief that blocks us from being complete, whole happiness.

The Act of Invocation: You invoke this invocation through writing a sacred letter to the Supreme Consciousness within your heart asking that the beauty of the woman within your heart flow into life. Ask that your heart open. Ask that all issues and experiences that keep the heart locked fall away with each conscious breath.

You will also need to choose a group of invocations or seven individual invocations that will further empower you to let go of issues that block you from sitting joyously and safely within your heart. It is vital that through the purification process to open the heart you focus on the action of conscious breathing. Resist getting caught up in the "I'm a victim, poor me" mentality as your issues begin to surface. Simply stay brave and focused, determined that you will become free of all fear, grief and resistance to love. This is such a sacred initiation, and it is the one that will introduce you to the compassion, wisdom and unconditional love of the Complete Earthly Woman.

Chapter 11

 Initiation 6
I Honor the Family

This initiation is a sacred and very powerful initiation, because at its completion you will fully accept all that you are as a person.

Purpose: Through the practice of this sacred initiation you will integrate the healing process of the inner child into a sacred union with the Complete Earthly Woman. The inner child will be both honored and nurtured though the invocation of the Supreme Consciousness within through a sacred union with the Complete Earthly Woman.

In this initiation you become the person you know yourself to be, the woman from within your heart, and you thank and step away from the victim and walk on empowered by the gifts that your life has given you. This life inspired you to seek your True self. This is the greatest gift you can ever receive.

The Act of Invocation: To invoke this initiation you need to practice the Honoring the Inner Child conscious breathing exercise in Chapter 6 until you feel that you are wholly connected. You also need to choose a group of invocations or seven individual invocations that will clear all issues based around interpretations of your childhood and your family, whether from your perspective as a mother, as a daughter or both.

Be prepared to exhale some grief, anger, suppression, frustration, fear or attachments. This is the initiation that will empower you to identify with your best attributes that came or come from you being part of your family.

You will know that this initiation is complete when your inner relationship with your family is one of truth, when you are comfortable, contented and inspired that you have been or are part of this family. Close this initiation with a letter you write to your family thanking them for their love and teachings and for bringing you into your body. This is not a letter they will ever see, but a letter that is written to the Supreme Consciousness. At the completion of this initiation you will move into your final initiation, ready as the Complete Earthly Woman.

∾   ∾   ∾

Initiation 7
I Honor My Duty

Within this initiation you will surrender all of your transformation to the beauty of giving love — not judgment — to all.

Purpose: This is the initiation that can complete your transformation into the Complete Earthly Woman or take you to the point at which you refused to grow. In this initiation you are required to live life giving love and understanding to all, a practice you access through the action of service and a constant flow of love. You will, within your own silence, speak to the Supreme Consciousness within and invoke love for all. You will nurture your new self in the act of giving divine wisdom to all situations. You will not allow any harshness within the minds of others to attack your sacred connection. You will set boundaries of love. This is done and measured by what you give out to others.

The Act of Invocation: To invoke this sacred initiation you must write to the Supreme Consciousness an agreement of heart service, invoking your commitment to give others love. This means in your job, your relationships, your home and every aspect of your life.

The key to the success of this initiation will be your capacity to discipline your thoughts, to work consciously, inhaling your truth. You will give service and kindness in the act of unconditional love and exhale all resistance. This is where you have met and become. Now you will walk your talk, always turning to the strength within to assist and guide you. All of your inner connections will be strong at this point and all of your initiations active. It is your duty in this initiation to honor your transformation through your commitment to honoring others. You will either help people within the community or within your family actively or silently by constantly invoking love for all within your heart.

Consciously accept that in your commitment to yourself and your values you heal our society by nurturing our children in the capacity of the Complete Earthly Woman. Through your actions within yourself and toward others you will further assist in healing Mother Earth and all that takes place upon her precious soil.

You will fully activate and complete this initiation when passing test after test after test and becoming more empowered, more empowered, more empowered. You are and will remain all the beauty of the Complete Earthly Woman. You will know your tests; they will make you question yourself, your belief, your faith and your inner commitment, and they will challenge you to find inner silence.

You will know when you have passed this initiation because you will be in control, in love with yourself, empowered and wearing the innocence of a child upon your face.

You will smile the sacred wisdom of the Complete Earthly Woman.

In your connection and experience of higher consciousness, you will be a key in the uplifting of the whole of humanity. Congratulations in this moment. Close your eyes. Inhale. Feel the silence. Feel the warmth. Feel the thank you. For the honor of being in your life—*Complete Earthly Woman.*

∾   ∾   ∾

inhale	Self love	*exhale*
inhale	Is the essence of	*exhale*
inhale	What you are	*exhale*
inhale	As within this moment	*exhale*
inhale	You are the	*exhale*
inhale	Simplicity	*exhale*
inhale	Innocence	*exhale*
inhale	Love	*exhale*
inhale	Wisdom	*exhale*
inhale	Heartbeat	*exhale*
inhale	Of our Divine Universal light	*exhale*
inhale	Mother Earth	*exhale*
inhale	Our sacred mother	*exhale*
inhale	Gatekeeper of Supreme Consciousness	*exhale*
inhale	Welcome to the chamber	*exhale*
inhale	Truth	*exhale*
inhale	Welcome to the chamber	*exhale*
inhale	Ancient unconditional love	*exhale*
inhale	Welcome home	*exhale*
inhale	Within the heart of	*exhale*
inhale	The Complete Earthly Woman	*exhale*

Continuing Self-Empowerment

Following are particular conscious breathing exercises to further empower your transformation. These are techniques that have invoked profound results within the lives of those who have practiced them. Use these invocations as you have done when practicing the conscious breathing exercises in Chapter 3. The difference with the following exercises is that you can practice any one of them at any time. You can swap and change as often as you like and practice one after the other if you so desire.

The following Mother Earth meditation is used to connect to the true essence of the womb. This meditation will take you within the womb of Mother Earth, and through your conscious breathing you will inhale her essence, further attuning yourself to your heart. I always refer this meditation to any women who are experiencing physical disease or discomfort within the sexual organs or lower part of the body. Through the process of this meditation and connecting to the womb of Mother Earth you will re-create the energy in your own womb, re-creating any imbalances, almost as if you nourish yourself through Mother Earth's divine wisdom and energy.

Mother Earth Meditation

In the following meditation or relaxation exercise, you will be connecting to yourself through conscious breathing, color and imagery to the four elements: fire, earth, water and air. In working consciously with these elements, you will merge within the beauty of Mother Earth and be empowered by her healing power.

To receive maximum benefits from this meditation, I suggest that you tape yourself reading it slowly and peacefully and listen to yourself guiding you through this process. Listening to your own voice is an incredibly effective and powerful healing tool, a simple and yet beneficial way to reprogram the subconscious mind. It is also an effective way in which you can reprogram the energy within the cellular memory of the body, as listening to and guiding yourself becomes a process or experience that is initiated and completed in your energy, in your oneness.

At the appropriate stages of the meditation, you can add different invocations that you are working on from Chapter 3. Alternate them as you shift through different layers of the physical, mental and emotional bodies. Doing this will further empower your transformation. When you record yourself reading through the meditation, remember to replace "you" and "your" with "I" and "I am" in the appropriate places so you are always speaking to yourself. If you are unable to tape yourself, then simply read through the meditation. Guide yourself through, silently creating the pictures in your mind, or have another person read you through the process. Either way will be incredibly effective.

Just remember, the most important thing is that you deserve to connect to the highest aspect of your feminine side and the magnificent qualities and gifts that await within. If you allow yourself freedom and the opportunity of this experience, transformation and inner union can happen to you. Have fun and enjoy.

Sit comfortably on the floor and begin breathing deeply, in through your nose and out through your mouth. Inhale peacefully as you create a rhythm in your breath similar to that of your heartbeat. Inhale deeply in through your nose and out through your mouth.

In your mind create a picture of a sparkling, bubbling brook. Look into the water of the brook, see it glistening in the sunshine. Notice the water swirling and pooling with the current of the small waterfalls that bubble over each rock. Listen to the sacred sound of the forest as the crickets hum the choir of nature and the water swirls and sings in melody.

As your eyes ponder the brook, you see a rock sitting amongst the swirling pools. Slowly you walk to the rock, climbing gently, peacefully into the water. The water is cool; immediately you feel calm. You begin to inhale deeply in through your nose and out through your mouth, consciously participating and being aware of each breath.

Bending down, you cup your hands, and they fill with water. You wash your face; the water is so cool, stimulating yet peaceful. You continue to wash your head, your chest; the coolness is so peaceful and calming. You feel centered, you breathe in calmness, and now your breath is altering and you are beginning to merge in oneness with Mother Earth.

You feel the coolness on your legs and you continue to breathe long, deep breaths. Now as you approach this warm, comfortable rock, you sit upon it with your feet in the water. They are caressed by the cool, flowing water. You close your eyes and merge in breath with the melody of nature.

Your skin is warmed by the sun and your feet

cooled by the water. You feel the trees nurturing you like nature's umbrella.

With your eyes closed you see a pink ray of light come from the trees and completely surround you. With each breath you begin to inhale this pink light, affirming to yourself with each breath: "I inhale each breath within my heart as Mother Earth turns the key within my heart."

Continue to inhale this opening of the heart in this divine pink light, calmly with each breath.

As you sit calmly breathing, you see a blue light emerge from you and point above the tallest tree. Begin to exhale all discomforts: fear, sadness, memories—everything that discomforts you. Create a picture—a sentence, a symbol, a word—and exhale this picture into the blue light with each breath.

As you exhale the last breaths of your picture a most magnificent golden light appears. It completely surrounds you. You inhale this golden light; it fills the water, and it fills you. This is your inner truth from your highest aspect. Inhale this truth, welcome it in, as the love within your heart begins to flow as the water with which you are one. Feel this golden light flow through you.

Look up. There are balloons everywhere, pink and gold, popping like little crackers in celebration of your oneness with Mother Earth. Inhale the light, the pink and golden light that fills these balloons. Feel your inner child giggle. See your inner child jumping in amongst the balloons that tumble down and pop around you. The inner child is nurtured in the fun and vibration of love that fills these balloons—the love that you inhale.

Right now, in this moment, as an adult, as a child, you are one with Mother Earth. Feel this moment, merge with it, be it. Feel and know your own silence and inner joy. This moment is your truth. Carry this moment with you. This is you, the woman connected to Mother Earth.

Carry this moment with you into each breath. This is you, the woman, the Complete Earthly Woman, connected with the spirit of Mother Earth.

ᘜ   ᘜ   ᘜ

Exhaling Female Blockages

For this exercise you will need to sit down in front of a mirror.

Begin by inhaling deeply and peacefully exhaling. Allow your breath to relax your body and calm your mind. Inhale deeply and peacefully exhale. As you inhale, repeat the following in your mind to the rhythm of each inhale:

I am a balanced integrated woman.

Repeat to yourself with each exhale:

I surrender all blockages of my female union.

As you repeat these invocations, quicken your breath. It is important throughout this exercise to remain focused on breathing. Inhaling and exhaling while consciously quickening your breath.

Breathe quick enough to remain comfortable, not too fast. You do not want to breathe and feel dizzy or lightheaded. Simply keep your breath quicker than normal and at an even flow. Continue to inhale and exhale, centering your awareness on your physical comfort. Are you experiencing any physical discomfort, or are you being challenged by the mind? The mind might be suggesting that you are destined to fail this exercise and not receive any benefits. I will give you an example. I practiced this technique with a woman who wanted to lose weight, which was the baggage of sexual abuse. As her breath quickened, her left nostril felt blocked. She then experienced a pain in her left nostril. The pain became quite intense, and it spread into her left eye. She continued to breathe, challenged by this pain. Finally she passed through this pain, and she knew that she had done so when she took one perfect, even, painless breath. She said that she had breathed through the vision of her female beauty that was stored in her left eye. She felt that after this day she was empowered to see herself differently, which in turn empowered her physical transformation.

This is what you have to do. Continue to breathe through all discomfort. You will know that you have finished the exercise, because your breath will become empty. There will be no physical discomfort and the mind will be silent.

Nurturing the Male

For this exercise, you will need to sit down in front of a mirror. Begin inhaling deeply and peacefully exhaling. Allow your breath to relax your body and calm your mind. Inhale deeply and peacefully exhale. As you inhale, repeat the following in your mind to the rhythm of each inhale:

I am a balanced integrated woman.
I am a balanced integrated woman.

Stare into your eyes in the mirror. Breathe deeply in through your nose and out through your mouth. Stare at your face, the structure of your face. Stare at your nose, your forehead and the shape of your face. Look for the male within you. See him in your face.

Continue to inhale deeply and exhale deeply, conscious of each breath you take. Now look into your eyes again and see him looking back at you. Keep your eyes centered and your breathing constant. Look for him, his interpretation of your life. In your heart invite him to let go. Invoke him within your breathing to let go, to release what he holds within that is not balanced in union with his divine female partner—your inner female.

As you continue to inhale, begin to inhale the words *thank you*. When you exhale, exhale *I let go with each breath.* Inhale—*thank you*; exhale—*I let go with each breath.* Continue until you feel in touch with what he is telling you. When you know you are in touch, then you can assist by consciously letting go of what he exhales and releases.

If you have ever been violated as a woman, your inner male will be carrying fears of protection, anger and inadequacies. Hold him in your heart, in your tears, caressing him as a child within your heart. As you inhale your empowered state and the connection that you have made, continue to thank him in each breath.

Remember that when you experience any type of release at all, it is important to stay centered. Continue to stare into your eyes, remaining consistent and disciplined in the repetition of your invocations and breathing. It is this determination that will allow what you will call forward to take place and truly leave. In your centered stare and constant breathing you are determined to have your experience, know that if you pull away, you are pulling away to say, "Poor me."

Looking at the sacred aspect of yourself—your beloved male—hold his hand and feel wholly comforted that today you are one on this sacred journey. He is the sacred aspect that will merge and is merging in the melodies of ecstasy and blissful love with the female. Together in union they are the essence of the Complete Earthly Woman.

Physical Health and Well-being—Conscious Breathing Invocation

This invocation is for the purpose of aligning your physical health to the essence of well-being. It is particularly appropriate to use this invocation to lose weight, heal addictions or heal disease, physical or mental. This will help create an all-over inner peace and harmony in your life. Practice just as you do your seven chosen invocations.

For this exercise you will need to sit in front of a mirror. As you focus on your vision, begin to inhale deeply and exhale. Allow your breath to relax your body and calm your mind. Through your conscious, controlled breathing, inhale peace. Through your conscious, controlled breathing, exhale all resistance. Continue this breathing until you feel that you are ready to begin the following:

INVOKE: *I am perfect physical harmony*

inhale	I am this heartbeat
exhale	**I exhale all resistance**
inhale	I am perfect synchronicity
exhale	**I exhale all resistance**
inhale	within the connection of each organ
exhale	**I exhale all resistance**
inhale	I am harmonized male and female energy
exhale	**I exhale all resistance**
inhale	I am physical, mental and emotional freedom
exhale	**I exhale all resistance**

INVOKE: *With each breath I inhale synchronicity with this heartbeat*

inhale	My life is the rhythm of this heartbeat
exhale	**I exhale all resistance**
inhale	I am the light and Supreme Consciousness
exhale	**I exhale all resistance**
inhale	within this heart
exhale	**I exhale all resistance**
inhale	I am the rhythm of my existence
exhale	**I exhale all resistance**

INVOKE: *With each breath each organ is the action of perfect synchronicity*

inhale	I am perfect immune balance
exhale	**I exhale all resistance**
inhale	I am perfect renal balance
exhale	**I exhale all resistance**
inhale	I am perfect iron balance
exhale	**I exhale all resistance**
inhale	I am perfect endocrine balance
exhale	**I exhale all resistance**
inhale	I am perfect skeletal balance
exhale	**I exhale all resistance**
inhale	I am perfect hormonal balance
exhale	**I exhale all resistance**

 INVOKE: *With each breath my inner female and inner male remain balanced as one*

inhale	I am divine female
exhale	**I exhale all resistance**
inhale	I am divine male
exhale	**I exhale all resistance**
inhale	I am divine sexual ecstasy of this sacred union
exhale	**I exhale all resistance**
inhale	I am humble in my expression
exhale	**I exhale all resistance**
inhale	of this sacred man and woman
exhale	**I exhale all resistance**

INVOKE: **With each breath I am physical, mental and emotional freedom**

inhale	I am physical peace, strength and well-being
exhale	**I exhale all resistance**
inhale	I am mental peace, strength and discipline
exhale	**I exhale all resistance**
inhale	I am emotional peace, strength and balance
exhale	**I exhale all resistance**

Honoring the Inner Child—Conscious Breathing Invocation

I suggest that you sit down in front of the mirror for this process. As you focus on your vision, begin to inhale deeply and exhale. Allow your breath to relax your body and calm your mind. Through your conscious, controlled breathing, inhale peace. Through your conscious, controlled breathing, exhale all resistance. Continue this breathing until you feel that you are ready to begin the following:

 INVOKE: **My life is an experience of a creative, peaceful, joyous inner child**

inhale	Sacred inner child union
exhale	**I exhale all resistance**
inhale	I am this union
exhale	**I exhale all resistance**
inhale	I live this union
exhale	**I exhale all resistance**
inhale	I experience this union
exhale	**I exhale all resistance**
inhale	My life reflects this union
exhale	**I exhale all resistance**

inhale	I am safe being a child
exhale	**I exhale all resistance**
inhale	The beauty in becoming a woman
exhale	**I exhale all resistance**
inhale	The wisdom in the connection
exhale	**I exhale all resistance**
inhale	of the woman and the child
exhale	**I exhale all resistance**
inhale	I am an expression of abundant creativity
exhale	**I exhale all resistance**
inhale	I am pure innocence
exhale	**I exhale all resistance**
inhale	I am the love of all and everything
exhale	**I exhale all resistance**

Practicing this invocation will empower your self-transformation, because you will be nurturing and transforming the little girl within this process.

Returning to Self-Power

In this visualization and conscious breathing exercise you are taking yourself consciously back into your self-power. It is both simple and effective and can be practiced anywhere. Through this process you will be able to consciously return to your self-power, as soon as you realize that you are struggling and removed from it. I have taught many women to invoke this visualization as often as required throughout a day and always to practice it when they are faced with making difficult decisions. It is the visualization to learn and use as often as you drink water.

In your mind create a platform of light. This platform symbolizes standing within your power. This platform exists within your heart and is your humble post. Begin to inhale deeply, in through your nose, while repeating to yourself the following: *I am inner truth. I exhale all resistance.*

As you inhale and exhale see yourself appear inside your heart. See yourself standing on your inner platform. With each breath the vision of yourself will become clearer and your connection to this visualization stronger. When you arrive at your platform you are integrated within your breathing to your inner power.

Each time that you slip into the "passenger's seat," lose self-confidence or lack the ability to reassure yourself with spiritual direction, it is time to step back into your self-power. This can be done quickly and effectively with this conscious breathing exercise.

The more situations and experiences you interpret and participate in while consciously existing in your self-power, the more growth and healing takes place.

This section and the exercises given here are provided to maintain your transformation to self-empowerment. Similar to a maintenance program. These exercises can be both practiced alone and with others. Where you can either be guided or guide another through any of the exercises provided.

From my heart I give to you the knowing within this book that self-transformation is a delight that will open the heart, transform the mind and empower your life. Allow it to happen and fill your heart with the action of self-love.

Genie O'Malley, author and speaker, is dedicated to helping others transform their daily lives through a natural process of self-awareness and, more importantly, self-acceptance. Her unique approach provides an astonishingly simple and effective gateway to the genuine, joyful and abundant life so many of us are looking for. She is also the author of *Balloons of Joy* and *The Breath Within Balloons of Joy: Conscious Breathing and Relaxation for Children and Young Adults*. O'Malley, from Australia, now lives in the U.S. with her husband, Christian, and their two children.

$\mathcal{N}$otes & Invocations

*N*otes & Invocations

Notes & Invocations

*N*otes & Invocations

$\mathcal{N}$otes & Invocations

*N*otes & Invocations

Notes & Invocations

otes & Invocations

Notes & Invocations

Notes & Invocations

Notes & Invocations

Notes & Invocations